D1501043

SEP 05 2014

beginner, *Rewrite* is full of tips, techniques, and
nd improve the way you revise your scripts. Not only do
sh to perfection your existing script, his explanations,
.... help you write your *next* script without the false starts,
detours, and wasted time that frustrate so many scribes. Highly recommended!"

— Jody Wheeler, writer and director, *The Dark Place*; producer, *Judas Kiss*

"Paul reminds screenwriters across the spectrum of the key processes of storytelling
that connect them with their audience, and he does it in a comforting and down-to-
earth way."

— Ben Lewin, writer and director, *The Sessions*

"I have known Paul Chitlik for more than thirty years. Paul has forgotten more about
the art of writing than most people ever know. This book is a wealth of information
for the writer who is going it alone, who gets no help from network or studio execs,
editors or producers, and directors. Paul understands that the true art of writing is
rewriting, and has fashioned an invaluable resource for anyone who truly wishes to
understand what it takes to be a writer in today's market."

— Joel Zwick, director, *My Big Fat Greek Wedding*, *Fat Albert*, and many TV episodes

"Creativity is a gift we all have; it's the writing and thus the rewriting we all have to
do, getting it in a script and on the screen that will make you turn to this book for
guidance."

— Quinn K. Redeker, co-writer, *The Deer Hunter*

"The old adage about writing holds true: get it down, then get it right. When you're
staring at a script that you thought was going to be great and for some reason
just isn't working, this book — clear, clever, succinct — will help you get it right."

— Graham Yost, writer, *Speed*, *Band of Brothers*, *The Pacific*, and others

"A master class in revision, written by a master craftsman. The book is essential for all
writers whether beginner or seasoned professional. The new material in the second
edition will only add to the book's excellent reputation. Chitlik's excellent work
embodies what so many books in our field lack — heart, soul, and a reverence for the
art and craft of writing and for writers."

— Jeffrey Davis, chair, Screenwriting Department, School of Film & TV,
Loyola Marymount University

"The book is more than good, it nails the process. Chitlik augments his theories on
rewriting in this elevated second edition of his venerable book, *Rewrite*, and goes
beyond by applying his theories to the ever-evolving demands of new media.
Fast becoming an industry standard, *Rewrite*, second edition, is a welcome and
needed addition to any screenwriter's library."

— Ernie Contreras, author, *Fairy Tale: A True Story*, *The Pagemaster*,
and HBO's *Walkout*

"Owning Paul Chitlik's *Rewrite* is like having a really smart, experienced writing
partner at your disposal 24/7. What writer wouldn't want that?"

— Ross Brown, assistant professor, Film and Media Arts, Chapman University;
author, *Byte Sized Television: Create Your Own TV Series for the Internet*

"I am a very lucky guy. I had the great fortune to be a student in not one but two of Paul Chitlik's very popular UCLA screenwriting classes where he brilliantly guided me toward creating a couple of the best scripts I've ever written. Paul's methods are responsible for helping me to grow as an artist in immeasurable ways. Paul is a pro's pro, and teaches exactly what it takes to perfect the ever trickier task of writing screenplays that excite studios, networks, and producers in every corner of Hollywood. *Rewrite* is like taking a Paul Chitlik master class, only he's made himself available to you at a moment's notice. I'm so impressed with *Rewrite* that I've made it required reading for numerous screenwriting classes that I teach in Point Park University's Cinema and Digital Arts Department. I highly recommend this wonderfully expanded and updated edition of *Rewrite* to anyone who hopes to see their work rise to the top of every producer's must-have list of scripts. Get *Rewrite*, study it, apply it to your next set of rewrites, and you just may achieve immortality on screens large and small."

— Steve Cuden, co-creator, *Jekyll & Hyde: The Musical*; animation teleplay writer; author, *Beating Broadway: How to Create Stories for Musicals That Get Standing Ovations*

"All writing is re-writing and Paul Chitlik proves in the second edition, that even re-writing a book on re-writing can be a winning formula. The first edition is excellent... the second even more so."

— Matthew Terry, filmmaker, screenwriter, teacher, reviewer, *www.microfilmmaker.com*

"*Rewrite* by Paul Chitlik is a step-by-step guide for screenwriters to take the first draft of their screenplay and greatly improve it. Chitlik states that screenplays often go through several rewrites before a final draft is achieved. He gives some very practical tips on how to make this process effective.

Chitlik covers two types of story structure and what types of stories they fit best: the three-act structure and the mythic structure often associated with Joseph Campbell. He then outlines how to develop your story's characters. I loved the chapter on the emotional relationship in the story. There's a chapter on effectively eliminating pages from your script to tighten the story without losing any of the most vital parts. Each chapter includes assignments for you to work on as you're reading so that ideally you're completing a rewrite of a script in the course of reading the book. There are ample examples from well-known movies throughout go illustrate Chitlik's points.

Rewrite is an invaluable resource for writers to tighten their scripts and make them better."

— Tom Farr, blogger
tom-farr.blogspot.com/2013/05/review-of-rewrite-second-edition-by.html

"Chitlik takes conventional wisdom and organizes it in a neat, step-by-step manner for the reader with exercises designed to make one's first draft more presentable."

— Jason T. Carter, blogger, *The Writer's Journey*

"Essential tools for every writer. Chitlik understands the processes of creating all aspects of storytelling, and teaches what every writer needs: to be their own editor in order to produce their best work."

— Dave Watson, editor, Movies Matter, *www.davesaysmoviesmatter.com*

PAUL CHITLIK

REWRITE

A STEP-BY-STEP GUIDE TO

STRENGTHEN STRUCTURE, CHARACTERS,
AND DRAMA IN YOUR SCREENPLAY

2nd Edition

WILLARD LIBRARY, BATTLE CREEK, MI

Published by Michael Wiese Productions
12400 Ventura Blvd., #1111
Studio City, CA 91604
tel. 818.379.8799
fax 818.986.3408
mw@mwp.com
www.mwp.com

Cover Design: Johnny Ink
Book Layout: Gina Mansfield Design
Editor: Pamela Grieman

Printed by McNaughton & Gunn, Inc., Saline, Michigan
Manufactured in the United States of America

© 2013 Paul Chitlik
All rights reserved. No part of this book may be reproduced in any form or
by any means without permission in writing from the publisher, except for
the inclusion of brief quotations in a review.

Library of Congress Cataloging-in-Publication Data

Chitlik, Paul, 1947-
 Rewrite : a step-by-step guide to strengthen structure, characters, and drama
in your screenplay / Paul Chitlik. -- Second edition.
    pages cm
 ISBN 978-1-61593-157-6 (pbk.)
1. Motion picture authorship. 2. Editing. I. Title.
PN1996.C54 2013
808.2'3--dc23
                          2013016170

Printed on recycled stock
Publisher plants ten trees for every one tree used to produce this book.

WILLARD LIBRARY, BATTLE CREEK, MI

For Sophia,
who taught me what love is.
And for Beth,
who showed me
how happy it could make me.

TABLE OF CONTENTS

Acknowledgments viii

Note on Gender viii

Introduction to the First Edition ix

Introduction to the Second Edition xiv

1 • Clarifying Story and Structure for Impact 1

2 • The Alternative Structure (Mythic Structure) 15

3 • The Powerful Protagonist 23

4 • The Central Emotional Relationship 41

5 • The Worthy Antagonist 45

6 • Ensuring Dynamic Scenes and Sequences 51

7 • Dialogue: Text, Subtext, and No Text 63

8 • Making Descriptions Leap off the Page 71

9 • Life Support for Your Protagonist 79

10 • Paring It Down 85

11 • Where Am I? 117

12 • The Right Look 121

13 • Finishing 129

14 • Applying Rewrite Techniques to Webisodes,
     Television, Comics, Graphic Novels, Games,
     and Other Media Yet to Be Discovered 135

Appendices

A • The Seven Points of *Thelma & Louise* 141

B • The Seven Points of *Ratatouille* 142

C • The Seven Points, More or Less, of *Pirates of the Caribbean* ... 144

D • The Beat Sheet of *In Good Company* 146

E • *Alien Abduction* — The First Sequence
and How It Developed 153

Bibliography 197

About the Author 199

Index 200

ACKNOWLEDGMENTS

Teachers often learn more from their students than vice versa, and I thank all my students for what they have taught me. I especially thank one, Terry Holdredge, for encouraging me to write the first edition of this book. He even went so far as to outline my lectures and give me a preliminary table of contents. The pressure!

I also want to thank Jim Schmerer, Richard Walter, Stephanie Moore, and Hal Ackerman of UCLA for their encouragement, support, and words of wisdom. Thanks go to my crew of trusted advisers for this project — Erica Byrne, Marty Winkler, Elizabeth Hargreaves, and Carri Karuhn. They helped me shape the book and improved its usefulness. Of course, anything they didn't catch or any mistakes I insisted on making anyway are my own fault.

More general career thanks go to Jeffrey Davis, Loyola Marymount University; Linda Venis, UCLA Extension; Marc Sheffler, king of the instant joke; Espresso Time (my second office); Star Frohman, who always forced me to go deeper; Barbara Alexander, agent extraordinaire; my publishers Michael Wiese and Ken Lee; and my incredibly correct, meticulous, and understanding editor, Pamela Grieman. Also, thanks to Gina Manfield whose exceptional design has made this book stand out on writers' bookshelves everywhere.

All unattributed quotes were taken from the Writers Guild of America, West conference, held in Los Angeles, California in 2008. I want to thank all the writers for sharing their expertise so that others may profit from their wisdom.

NOTE ON GENDER

To avoid confusion, I have usually used the masculine set of pronouns when I write about characters within a movie in general. Of course, when they are specifically female characters, I use the feminine set. When writing about readers, producers, writers, development executives, agents, and studio personnel in general, I have used the feminine set of pronouns. It's understood that any of these roles can be played by either gender.

INTRODUCTION
TO THE FIRST EDITION

All professional screenwriters, and most experienced amateurs, know that no script is ready to shoot after only one draft. It's not at all unusual for a script to go through a dozen or more drafts (I marked upwards of thirty on one of my own projects) before it gets to the set, and even then it's not finished. Most professionals wading through the rewrite process, though, have people guiding them: other writers, executive producers and producers, development executives, agents, and managers. But new writers don't have the support system to get them from the "puke draft" to one that is of professional quality and ready to submit.

Beginning screenwriters can refer to Syd Field's *Screenplay*, Blake Snyder's *Save the Cat*, or Chris Vogler's *The Writer's Journey*, to name but three of scores of books available to learn the basics of screenwriting. But the real application of craft comes in the rewrite. Only a few books offer any help to the rewriter. Problem is, none is a how-to book that gives specific step-by-step instructions to the novice writer. None offers a complete, practical approach that guides you through the complete process. Film schools that offer rewriting classes (few schools do) are at a loss for texts. Individuals are on their own.

Rewrite, second edition, is the new writer's practical guide to getting through the next draft of his or her screenplay. From self-assessment to restructuring to revoicing, it charts an easy-to-follow, task-specific course through the miasma of the rewrite process. Citing examples of well-known movies and providing periodic "to do" assignments, this book makes the difficult journey a little less lonesome and a lot less foreboding. *Rewrite* serves as your development executive, your instructor, and your trusted adviser to guide you through the rewrite process in the absence of direct feedback.

In my nearly thirty years as a television and film writer, producer, and director, and my twelve years teaching at UCLA and Loyola Marymount

University, I have rewritten literally hundreds of teleplays and screenplays and supervised the writing and rewriting of another 1,500-plus. Here's the first thing I learned about writing: Writing is hard. The second thing I learned: It's not done until it's rewritten. Yes, the torture of getting it down on paper, of facing the blank monitor, is over when you've finished the first draft. You can sit back and feel the warmth of "having written" flow over you. Problem is, because you're not sure of yourself or the process, you don't know what to do next, and that's why desk drawers everywhere are full of manuscripts that will never see the light of day again.

But now it's time to take the diamond in the rough, the block of granite that you have carved out of the quarry of your mind, and turn it into the Star of India or the Pietà. Or, to drop the metaphors, you can take all that ink and paper of your first draft and recycle it because chances are you won't be able to sell it as is. Or you can possibly turn it into *Chinatown* or *Shakespeare in Love* or *The Life of Pi*.

Let's look at it another way. More than 70,000 projects a year are registered by the Writers Guild of America, West. But studios and production companies (I'm not talking about your friend with the new HD video camera) make only 350 or so films a year. And I can say with absolute certainty that not a single one of them is the real first draft. Every single one was rewritten by the original writer at least once, more likely a dozen times, and quite possibly others have worked it over as well. So the truth is, to go from the 70,000 to the 350, you must pass through rewrite-ville.

But rewrite-ville is not a bad place to be. As a matter of fact, according to writer-director Jane Anderson, writer of *When Billie Beat Bobbie, It Could Happen to You*, and *The Positively True Adventures of the Alleged Texas Cheerleader-Murdering Mom*, "It's inevitable that the first draft is a shitty draft." She even goes so far as to recommend writing a terrible first draft on purpose: "It's not a flaw, but part of the process."

This is where the fun can be. This is where, as my friend Vince McKay asserts, "The magic begins." Or, as a student of mine maintains, "This is where the work begins." This is where those great turns of phrase come from. This is where writers choose to tell about character and not just plot information. Jim Schmerer, who created and supervised UCLA's online Professional Program in Screenwriting for many years and whose television credits range from *Star Trek* to *MacGyver* and way too many more to mention, points out that in *Outbreak*, Laurence Dworet and Robert Roy Pool, the credited writers, have Dustin Hoffman's character need information from the Coast Guard. A secretary tells him that she has a friend who's in the Coast Guard. In the first draft, Hoffman might have said, "Could you ask him to help?" and that would convey all the information he needs. But he says, "How good a friend?" In the final draft, the secretary answers, "Better than his wife would like," which tells us not only that she can get the information but also something about her character.

That's the kind of double hit you can create in rewriting that, while you're buzzing through a first draft, you don't have time to think about.

But there's much, much more craft involved. Now's the time to see if what you had in mind got put down on the page. Now's the time when you take the block of granite and chip away at everything that isn't the Pietà. Now's when you hone and polish, expand and contract, build and shape. It's more fun now that the page isn't blank. It's more thoughtful and artful. But if you don't have a mentor, a studio executive, or a director to give you "notes," where do you start?

You start with this book. With your screenplay on one side of the desk and this book on the other, you follow a clear process that will help you analyze your screenplay, identify strengths and weaknesses, and create a course of action, a blueprint, for your rewrite.

A truism of screenplay writing is that rewriting is hard. Rewriting on your own is even harder. *Rewrite* is like having your own rewrite mentor so you don't have to go through the process by yourself. Each chapter has a "To Do" section offering practical exercises that relate directly to your current screenplay but that also give you a method to use in the future. For best results, do them as you go along, but feel free to read the whole book through before writing anything new.

The order I have set out in this book is the order I suggest to my students, but just as every writer approaches the rewrite from a different angle, doing different things in different orders, you can read and use this book any way that suits you.

One rule about screenwriting — there are no rules. There are conventions that have worked for a hundred years in film (and 2,500 years before that in playwriting), but there are no rules. So, if at any point you disagree with me, do what you feel is best and see if it works. If it does, good. If it doesn't, try it my way and see what you get. Chances are it'll work my way, because my way isn't my way; it's the way most screenwriters and development executives in Hollywood approach the screenplay today.

Which brings up another issue. We're talking about Hollywood movies here. We're not talking about *Jules et Jim, Shoot the Piano Player, Los Olvidados, Belle Epoch*, or *The Apu Trilogy*. Of course, some of what I'm about to lay out here works for those films, but not everything. I don't know how to write for French New Wave cinema, Italian Post-War Neorealism, Spain pre- or post-Franco, or India after the Raj. They're good films that continue to touch the lives of their moviegoers, and even us lowly Americans, but they're foreign to most American audiences in structure, approach, and content, and so, unacceptable to most Hollywood studios and production companies. And, I assume, the goal is to make a film that American studios will buy and American audiences will appreciate.

If, however, the goal is to make the best indie film out there, you'll still do better rewriting your film with my guidelines than trying to copy the form of *Last Year at Marienbad* (even if you could figure it out, and I couldn't and I read the book!). A good indie film still needs good structure, good characters, good dialogue, good action. Have a look at *Moonlight Kingdom* for a good example.

So let's get started on that rewrite.

But wait. How long is this process going to take? If you have no other responsibilities and can work full time on it, it could take from a few weeks to a couple of months. If you have a job and a family, maybe three to four months working ten hours per week. Adjust your time frame accordingly.

Writers are notorious for procrastinating. I suggest you do the same, but with a plan. I usually straighten out my office, vacuum the house, go for a bike ride, and take in the dry cleaning. Whatever you're going to do, write it down, then do it. Don't add to the list. When you've finished, you're ready. Mind clear, spirit willing. Then come back to chapter one.

INTRODUCTION
TO THE SECOND EDITION

Movies as an art form are constantly changing. So much so, as a matter of fact, that the term *films* is really no longer applicable, or rarely applicable, as many, if not most, movies are now shot, posted, and distributed on digital video. Just as movies change, so do my ideas about movies. While the observations I made about movie structure in the first edition of this book are still valid, I have come to some new conclusions about subplots and point of view. And there has been an explosion of delivery tools that has created new markets and formats for writers. So this new and updated second edition represents my latest thoughts on the process of rewriting for movies and other media.

The first edition is now a staple in many film classes across the country and around the world. I frequently get fan email and Facebook postings from readers in such far-flung places as Moscow, Stockholm, and Bangkok! I've been summoned to the estate of one of the world's top box-office stars to discuss my views on structure and character. I've spoken in person to writers in Australia, Chile, Spain, Cuba, Italy, and France. Other professional writers tell me they refer to the book when they come to a dead end in their writing. One just informed me that he quoted me on movie structure in his new book. All this has been tremendously gratifying.

Yet some readers have had questions that weren't answered in the first edition, so I have expanded some chapters and written new ones. A chapter on the "The Central Emotional Relationship" explores the emotional side of your central character and the aspect of your film that most holds your audience's attention. A chapter on "The Alternative Structure" explains how mythic structure applies to certain films and how to use it for your film if it's a better fit than the traditional seven-point structure.

Of course I have added more examples, some of which are in current release, to ensure that readers will be familiar with them (while retaining examples that go back to the 1930s so that continuity in structure can be demonstrated). A new chapter dedicated to dialogue makes its debut, as does an expanded chapter on "Paring It Down," which now contains more specifics and an edited before-and-after scene.

Not only have movies changed since the publication of the first edition, but the whole concept of media has been broadened. While the Web was certainly on everyone's mind and in everyone's home and office when the first edition was published, now tablets and smartphones have joined computers as instruments on which to view media. This has created a whole new form (and format) with which to tell stories, so I have included a chapter on how to apply the concepts of this book to webisodes, comics, graphic novels, and other media that may be in the pipeline.

I have also expanded the appendices to include the structures of additional movies and sample pages for a television movie (the first ever shot in digital video and the first "found footage" movie) I wrote for Dick Clark Productions and UPN to follow the script through several rewrites.

Of course, new questions will come up as will new media and ways to use them (and please tell me about them), but I remain firm in my belief that story and characters are the fundamental things people want to watch, and that profound knowledge of story structure and character development will serve a writer in any medium.

I pored through hundreds of emails and a ton of notes from students from all over the world so that this edition of *Rewrite* would be the most complete and up-to-date tool kit.

It's powerful stuff.

Now it's time to get to work.

CLARIFYING STORY AND STRUCTURE FOR IMPACT

When a developer decides to build a skyscraper, one of the first things he does, after researching and selecting the site, is to hire an architect to design the structure. He knows that a builder, no matter how experienced or educated, can't construct a high-rise without blueprints. The blueprints will detail the entire project from the depth of the foundation to the size and color of the tiles in the men's room. The plans enable the hundreds of people working to realize the project to have the same vision, to be in agreement on process and result. Not that there isn't opportunity for change (if you've ever remodeled your house you know about change orders) or creative collaboration. But everyone works from a common plan.

In film and television, that common plan is the script. Everyone from the props person to the lead actor relies on that document for guidance, so it is a technical document as well as a literary one. And, just as with blueprints, there are certain conventions that everyone relies on. One is a reliance on story.

If movies are all about characters and their goals, what characters do when faced with barriers to these goals is the story. To define story in the simplest way: There's a person. He has a goal. There's a wall between him and the goal. He has to go over, under, around, or through the wall to get to his goal.

That's the story. That's the plot of your movie — the process of getting to the goal. The goal may change. The wall may take various forms (both inside your protagonist and outside of him). But the fact remains; story is the character striving towards his goal.

An expression of this form in dramatic terms has worked for thousands of years — the three-act structure. This has been refined in the last hundred years of movie making and can be summed up in seven specific points of your movie, all of which relate to the protagonist's goal.

This seems like the starting point for thinking about your movie, but it's not the only one. My philosophy, shared by thousands of other writers (but by no means all), is that movies begin with character. Of course, what befalls the character or what the character does in pursuit of his goal are what movies are about as well. But I chose to start the book by discussing structure because you can't discuss character without discussing structure, and I didn't want to have to define my terms twice.

I encourage you to flip back and forth between the chapters much like a professor would jump between subjects in a lecture. Remember that character is action; action is character. The very act of pursuing a goal is how you define your character. It's all intertwined.

So, let's see if your script has the seven points that provide the bare bones of the body of your movie. The points:

1. Ordinary life: getting to know who the central character is and what his issue (flaw) is. We see the protagonist in his usual surroundings, dealing with the usual people in his life, but we also see that he has some issues and that there is a need for change. He may or may not know that.

In *Thelma & Louise*, written by Callie Khouri, for example, Thelma (Geena Davis) starts off as the repressed housewife to car salesman, district manager Darryl (Christopher McDonald), a male chauvinist pig if there ever was one. She even has to ask his permission to go away for the weekend. Her first act of rebellion comes when Thelma calls Louise (Susan Sarandon) back and tells her the pick-up time.

This is a film full of montages. The first long one is of Thelma packing. But the point of this montage is to show her packing way too much stuff (which will lead to conclusions by the cop, Hal Slocumb, played by Harvey Keitel, much later) and to note that she packs a gun with distaste. How she handles the gun later will also demonstrate how far she's come on her journey.

Once she's in the car and has handed over the gun to Louise, she hears some fateful words: "You get what you settle for." Apparently, she's settled for Darryl. If she ever wants to get rid of him, we infer, she's got to do something about it. Her condition is clear. Her issues are clear.

Geena Davis, Thelma & Louise, *written by Callie Khouri, directed by Ridley Scott (Pathé Entertainment, 1991).*

We have no idea what we're in for while we watch the opening credits of *In & Out,* screenplay by Paul Rudnick. The location is set up by a series of local "beauty shots" as we're introduced to the "Great big small town" of Greenleaf, Indiana, that Howard Brackett (Kevin Kline) lives in. This is a heart-and-soul town, the kind of town that made America strong and rich, the kind where the values haven't changed since it was settled in the 1800s. Or so it would seem.

When we meet Howard, he's in the classroom, his milieu, reciting a Shakespearean sonnet. We can sense his enthusiasm for Shakespeare. He makes his students laugh. He tolerates their questions about a former student, Cameron Drake (Matt Dillon), who's up for an Academy Award'.

When a nervous student gives him a letter to open from Indiana University, we understand his level of commitment to his students, and his students' admiration of him. He's a likable guy. If we weren't already convinced, when his buddies shower him with champagne because of his upcoming wedding to Emily Montgomery (Joan Cusack), we're positive. Everyone likes Mr. Brackett.

Kevin Kline and Tom Selleck, In & Out, *written by Paul Rudnick, directed by Frank Oz (Paramount Pictures and Spelling Films, 1997).*

And everyone knows Howard's life is about to change, but they have no idea how much, and neither do we. We think he's about to get married to a woman he's been engaged to for years. She tries on her dress with Howard and his mother, Berniece (Debbie Reynolds).

But what's the issue? The issue is subtextual. Why has this purportedly heterosexual man not had sex with his fiancée of three years? Why has he not admitted that he's gay? Does he even know?

2. The inciting incident: usually around page 15 (or fifteen minutes into the film), give or take a couple of pages. Something happens to your protagonist that will change his life forever. Eventually, it will compel him to act. It will help him define his goal.

In *Thelma & Louise*, they stop at a country bar, and the drinking begins. Louise is a little hesitant, but Thelma reminds her, "You said we were gonna have some fun, so let's have some." Thelma starts dancing with a stranger who fills her full of beer and spins her until she's dizzy. When he takes her outside for some "air," he forces himself on her. Soon, it's a full-fledged rape and beating, eventually stopped by Louise pulling the trigger on Thelma's gun and putting a hole in the man's heart.

Now that's an inciting incident!

Their lives are definitely going to change now.

In *In & Out*, there are two events in town — Howard's imminent wedding and Cameron's Oscar* possibilities. These two converge during the Academy Awards* presentation itself when, after some very funny scenes from the war movie Cameron was nominated for and some insider jokes by Glenn Close, Cameron wins the award. In his acceptance speech, he thanks Howard, his high school drama teacher, and then says, quite without necessity, that the teacher is gay. In a gesture he thinks is a tribute, he dedicates the night to Howard Brackett. Things are never going to be the same for Howard Brackett again.

Emily, Howard's fiancée, is confused. "Howard, what's he talking about?" Of course, had she thought about it, she might have guessed. A three-year engagement devoid of sex. Barbra Streisand movies. Disco music. In the nutty world Rudnick has created, it all adds up.

Now the film has a purpose. Now it's rolling. Because that's what an inciting incident does — it changes the life of the protagonist forever. It forces him to seek a goal he may not have thought of or, if he had thought of it, never had the courage to pursue. In this case, it wreaks havoc on Howard's life. How can he get married if he's gay? It's news to his mother, his father, his fiancée. And Howard claims it's news to him, too. He's not gay, no no, not him. He's just about to get married for cryin' out loud.

3. End of act 1: when your character decides on a course of action in order to deal with whatever the inciting incident brought up. Usually, another major event forces him to decide that he must take action to reach a new goal. He creates a plan to help him reach that goal. This usually occurs between pages 25 and 35. Now your character has a goal, and your story has focus.

Thelma calls Darryl at four in the morning, and he isn't there. She starts to understand that maybe she's the one who should be upset about her spouse's behavior instead of vice versa. After Louise decides they should go to Mexico, Thelma has a conversation with Darryl, but he's too busy with his football game. He makes an idle threat, and she tells him to "go fuck yourself." Her attitude is changing.

Thelma decides to go to Mexico and learns about Louise's past run-in with the law in Texas. Now she asks how long will it take to get to Mexico. She states her goal. That's the end of act 1.

In *In & Out*, the pronouncement begins to create doubts in certain minds, but its ramifications are ominous when the principal, played by Bob Newhart, warns Howard to prove himself straight and get married. His students, the ones on his team, begin to doubt him and turn modest when he enters the locker room. Even his buddies at his own bachelor party are thrown for a loop. And then the priest counsels him to "be" with his fiancée. He rushes to Emily and tries to make love to her only to be freaked out by a Richard Simmons video. This inciting incident has created chaos in his life. He's got to do something about it. What? By the end of the act, Howard's mission is clear — he has to get married and prove that he's not gay.

4. Midpoint or turning point: wherein the action takes a sudden and new, unexpected direction. Yes, this does happen right around the middle wherein the action takes a sudden and new, unexpected direction. The goal may change. The central character may realize what his flaw is. His true *needs* become more important than what he *wants*.

Jimmy (Michael Madsen), Louise's boyfriend, is waiting for Louise at the hotel where he was supposed to wire her the money. She gives the money to Thelma for safekeeping, and we should know by now that something's going to go wrong with that, but we don't. When J.D. (Brad Pitt) comes to Thelma's door, all wet and seductive, Thelma takes him in and her life really changes. Darryl and she had been together since she was fourteen. He was the only man she had ever known. Now she learns a thing or two about sex with J.D. As a matter of fact, she's light-headed and drunk with sex the next morning. That is, until Louise asks her where the money is. J.D. has stolen it. Now the story spins off in a new direction. Thelma wants to maintain that "it's okay," but Louise says, "It's not okay. None of this is okay."

Up to this point, Thelma has been pulled along by events. She hasn't yet propelled the action by design, though what has happened to her has propelled the action. But now she has to take action. She takes charge. The action spins off in a new and unexpected direction. The women go on a crime spree!

Just before the middle of *In & Out*, Howard is still determined to prove that he is not gay. In a masterpiece visual, he literally bumps into the one person who can help him at, not coincidentally, a crossroads.

The catalyst for his self-discovery is Peter Molloy, played by Tom Selleck, an out-of-the-closet journalist who just won't let the story go. He forces Howard to come to terms with himself. How? By accidentally knocking him over at an intersection — literally the crossroads of his life. By kissing him full on the mouth and making him accept the fact that he likes it.

Now Howard's task is to come to grips with the fact that he's gay. The story spins off in a different direction. His goal is different.

5. The low point: end of the second act, the all-is-lost point in terms of the goal. It appears there's no way in hell he'll ever reach his goal. Happens around page 75–85 depending on the length of the script.

In *Thelma & Louise*, Darryl can't believe it when the FBI and Hal show him the tape of Thelma's convenience store robbery, but Thelma thinks she may have "found her calling" (armed robbery). Hal later questions J.D. and asks him if he thinks Thelma would have robbed the store if he hadn't stolen their money, and it's clear he thinks they're just victims of circumstance. When Louise and Thelma next call Darryl, Louise asks him to put the cops on, and Hal takes the phone. He wants them to turn themselves in to him; he knows they're going to Mexico.

This is the low point of the film, the end of the second act. Nothing's going well. Louise says the only thing they had going for them was that the cops didn't know where they were going. And now they know. They're frightened, but determined. They head off into the night.

Things are no better for Howard by now. He's finally at the wedding, still not owning up. At the altar, doubts creep in, and he admits to Emily, and to the world, that he's gay. He should be relieved, but he's not. He's flustered, confused. Peter congratulates him and gets clocked in the jaw for his trouble. Howard's life is over.

But the ultimate low point takes place off camera and Howard relates it to his father, who has come over after the aborted wedding. Howard's been fired because he's gay. Everything he had ever worked for is out the window. He's devastated the woman he loves (not in *that* way, but loves nonetheless). How's he ever going to regain his life?

6. The final challenge: when your protagonist sees something, hears something, or even remembers something that reanimates him and gives him the will to continue at the beginning of act 3. Then he prepares to face the final test, the final barrier that your character must overcome in order to reach his goal. The last, biggest battle. The run across Manhattan to proclaim his love. The final struggle to the summit. The last ten yards. This occurs very close to the end of your film.

Once Thelma and Louise have been located, their fate is sealed. Or appears to be. They could give themselves up, or they could turn and fight. But either way they'd lose, and neither way would be on their terms. If there's anything that Thelma's learned, it's that she now has control, and has to keep control, of her own life. She tells Louise she is a good friend. On the edge of the Grand Canyon, with no escape possible, Louise says she's not going to give up. Thelma suggests that they don't get caught. They should keep on goin'. She points to the edge of the canyon. Louise: "You sure?" Thelma: "Yeah." They kiss, start the car, hold hands, and fly into the canyon.

That's her final challenge, and she reaches her goal. She's completely free now. No one is telling her how to lead her life.

Howard Brackett should be receiving the teacher-of-the-year award, but now he can't because he's gay. But his family and his students and the rest of the community aren't about to let that happen, so in a Spartacus moment — "I am Spartacus. I am Spartacus" — everyone admits to being gay. Howard is vindicated for coming out, life returns to normal, and everyone is accepted for who they are.

Only problem is, Howard is not the agent of his own salvation. Yes, he came out, but he didn't really stand up for himself and fight the principal. His brother did. This is an example of having the cavalry make a last-minute rescue, and it's one of the failings of the film. Had Howard fought, the finish would have been much stronger.

7. The return to (the now changed forever) normal life: two or three pages to show us that life goes on and that our character has triumphed and changed.

It could be argued that there is no return to a now-changed-forever normal life in *Thelma & Louise*. They're dead. But what could be a greater change than that? The slide show of their journey underscores that they had the time of their lives. And now their lives are over. But Thelma went on an incredible journey of self-discovery and change. The implication is that it's the audience that is going to return to a now-changed-forever life because of Thelma and Louise's journey. They may never look at men in the same way again.

For Howard, there must be a moment of *normal gay life*. In this case, it's the renewal of vows that his parents make with him and his presumed "date," Peter (the newsman), looking on. There's no drastic external change. He'll still teach. He'll still be popular in town. It's just that he's gay now.

Guidelines, Not Laws

The seven points are only guidelines, of course. But the inciting incident should come as early as possible while still showing us who the main character is and why we should care about him. All points after that are in relation to the character's goal. (See Appendix A for a compressed version of the seven points of *Thelma & Louise*.)

There are scenes between these points — important scenes — and many barriers to get through and many people to relate to, but these are the major signposts along the way of your protagonist's journeys. I say journeys, because the story is only one of the journeys. The protagonist is really on three journeys: the A story — the plot; the B story — the relationship; and the C story — the internal journey dealing with the flaw. And every one of these stories has a seven-point structure. And every point along each of these journeys is defined in terms of the goal: reaching the story goal; creating or mending a relationship and thus reaching the emotional goal; changing into a better person (learning something about life that will help him), and thus reaching the personal development goal.

These journeys are intertwined and interdependent. Often, a plot point for the A story serves as the same point in the B or C story. In fact, the better integrated the three stories, the better the screenplay. More on these stories in future chapters.

To Do

Briefly outline your story in terms of the seven points. Write no more than a sentence about each of the seven points. Make sure that each point after the inciting incident relates to the goal of your central character.

When you've done all that, come back here. There's more to do on story.

The Beat Sheet

It's possible that your story is out of balance or is missing some of the points. Now's the time to determine where you are in your structure. Were all your points expressed in terms of the protagonist's goal? Were they in proximity to the balance described above? Now we're going to get intimate with your script. Without making any changes in your story yet, we need to see exactly what you have in terms of scenes, so let's write a beat sheet of your story.

If you're like most professional screenwriters, you didn't just sit down and start to write your screenplay. You thought about it, you wrote notes, you may have even done some character sketches. And, if you followed procedure, you at least did a beat sheet, if not a complete treatment (that's the subject of another book). A beat sheet is a list of the scenes of your story. Every writer does it differently, but most write at least a line or two to remind them what each scene will be (see Appendix B for a sample beat sheet). But the beat sheet you wrote when you started your script might not correspond to what ended up in your script. You may have added scenes, changed them, taken some away. That's the process. When you're writing the beat sheet, it's easy to shift scenes around, insert new ones, take out ones that don't really move the story.

When you do your rewrite, you've got to be ready to do this, too, so you need a new beat sheet to get the lay of the land. The best way to do this, according to some screenwriters, is to write each beat on an index card. Then shuffling is a cinch. Most screenwriting programs give you the ability to do the same thing, so you can choose. But whatever way you choose, it will help you to do that now. This will take some time, but don't worry, I'm patient. Come back when you've got a one-line description of each scene including who's in it, where they are, and what the conflict or character point is of that scene (more on what should be in a scene in chapter 7). Do not include transitions such as riding in a car or establishing shots. Number each beat for convenience. The beat sheet will probably be three single-spaced pages or so, with anywhere from thirty to seventy-five scenes. I'll wait here while you do that.

Developing Subplots

You're back. Good. Let's talk about subplots, because they're easier to talk about than to layer into your story. You should, by this time, be thinking of the two main subplots — that is, the B and the C story — the emotional subplot and the personal growth subplot. In most stories, the central story is the A story. In romantic comedies, it's the emotional, or B, story.

There are others, too, because there are always other things going on in a protagonist's life — he could have a story with the barista at the local Starbucks; there could be something happening with his dog; he might have an issue with his floor wax. These should reflect his main issue in some way, but don't necessarily have to.

The protagonist is not the only person in your movie. He has friends, lovers, enemies. Each of these people can have a subplot of his own. The more important supporting characters can have a story with the seven points, especially the antagonist. Lesser characters can have stories that merely have a beginning, middle, and end, so three story points are all that are needed. But the main issue here is, do the subplots somehow illuminate or reflect any of the central character's stories or issues? If they don't, you'll need to ask yourself why you need them.

Raising the Stakes

If the biggest, hardest barrier to your protagonist reaching his goal comes at the beginning of the story, where do you go from there? It would be all downhill and not very suspenseful. You've got to set up your story so that at each step, it gets harder and harder for your protagonist to get past the obstacles in his way. But there's more.

What is the penalty if your central character doesn't achieve a short-term and, eventually, the long-term goal? In other words, what are the stakes? What is the jeopardy for the protagonist? If he drives too fast, his car will slide off the road. If he fails a test, he'll have to start all over again. If he forces himself on the girl, he'll lose her.

Or his life.

The consequences of failure should be dire for your character. He could lose a fortune. He could lose his house, his children, or his job. The country or world could be destroyed. Whatever it is, it has to be worthy of our attention. Going after a goal that is not worthy will make your audience not care enough. If they don't care, they won't watch.

And as you progress in your script, you should be continually raising the stakes. Do you?

To Do

What happens to your central character if he fails in his quest? What are the consequences of failure? Write one or two lines describing the stakes.

The Barriers

Some words of reminder about barriers — they come from within and they come from without. The barrier within is your protagonist's flaw. It's what will prevent him from achieving his goal unless he overcomes it. So we need to be reminded what that flaw is, and we need to see it affect the outcome of attempts to overcome barriers. And it's best if we see it in the first visual of the protagonist.

In other words, you have to set up learning situations for your protagonist. Have you?

And it's best if we see it in the first visual of the protagonist. In other words, you have to set up learning situations for your protagonist. Have you?

Often, new writers will stop there, thinking the protagonist is also the antagonist: "She herself is the person who is preventing her from reaching her goal." But that is the case in *every* movie. The protagonist also must fight something outside of himself, during which he overcomes his own flaw.

So have you set up situations in which the antagonist force makes life difficult for your protagonist? Again, ask yourself, is it tough to reach the goal or is it easy? It had better be tough. The tougher the better.

Who Is the Real Hero?

One of the most difficult things about writing a feature film is to figure out who the hero is. Yes, hero. Even in a romantic comedy. Even in a teen sex romp. Even in a horror picture, there is a hero. The hero is the person who has to overcome adversity to reach his goal. And he must be the person who does this in the final challenge (sometimes called the climax). In other words, the main character must be the agent of his own salvation. The cavalry can't come riding in at the last minute (as it does in *Fort Apache*). His best friend can't save him. A virus can't save the world from Martian invaders (one of the main flaws of *War of the Worlds*). It has to be the protagonist — the hero — who fights and perseveres and overcomes whatever final barriers arise between him and his goal (Luke in *Star Wars*, Dorothy in *The Wizard of Oz*). If not, the audience will be unsatisfied. They might not know why, but they will not be happy with the movie.

To Do

Write in one line what your protagonist does to overcome the big barrier in the final challenge. He can have help, but he must lead the charge, whatever form that charge takes.

You've done some major work in this chapter, so it's time for a little reward. Think of something mindless that you don't ordinarily make time for. An hour reading the newspaper at Starbucks. Bowling a couple of frames. A trip to the library for no reason at all. I like to exercise after completing a stage in a rewrite, so I'd be on my mountain bike by now, challenging the Verdugo Hills. Go do something other than writing (or even thinking). Then come back.

THE ALTERNATIVE STRUCTURE (MYTHIC STRUCTURE)

I'm not the first one to point out that *Star Wars* (written by George Lucas) follows the paradigm of the mythic hero's journey delineated in Joseph Campbell's *The Hero with a Thousand Faces*. It became so well known in the industry that George Lucas used the mythic structure that Campbell's book became required reading for film critics and film analysts. Campbell himself became the subject of much attention outside of academia and even sat for a number of interviews with television journalist Bill Moyers. Linda Seger, in *Making a Good Script Great*, points out that the mythic tale of the hero can be broken down into ten points according to Campbell. She uses *Star Wars* to illustrate the point.

Let's look at *Star Wars*, then, as exemplifying another way to structure a film. Many of the plot points coincide, and I'll point that out as we go along. While I'll draw on Seger's analysis, I'll focus on a twelve-point structure, described in Christopher Vogler's book, *The Writer's Journey: Mythic Structure for Storytellers & Screenwriters*, to illustrate my points.

Just as in the movies we've discussed, Lucas opens with views of **ordinary life**. Of course, ordinary life in this case begins with Princess Leia (Carrie Fisher) being captured by the forces of the Empire. She sends a pair of androids on a mission to find Ben Obi-Wan Kenobi (Alec Guinness). Eventually, the droids end up at the farm where Luke Skywalker (Mark Hamill), his aunt, and his uncle live. This truly is ordinary life, far from the battles of the Imperial

Empire and the Rebel forces. Luke is itching to break away and train to be a pilot, but his prospects are bleak. This is step number 1.

Then, while cleaning R2-D2 (Kenny Baker), he receives a hint of his **call to adventure** (step 2) in the form of a hologram of Princess Leia asking Obi-Wan Kenobi for help. It's not the complete call at this stage, since the message is not complete. Not until he is rescued by Obi-Wan Kenobi does he finally hear the whole message. Kenobi then tries to recruit him for the mission he must undertake.

But Luke turns him down. This is the third stage, **the refusal of the call**. The fourth stage, wherein a **mentor encourages him to accept the call**, begins when Kenobi prevails upon him to take him at least partway to Alderaan. When Luke returns to his farm, he finds that stormtroopers have slaughtered his family. He decides **to cross the first threshold and enter the special world**. That's the fifth stage of the story.

Let's stop for a minute and look at this from the point of the view of the structure we've been discussing. Yes, we typically start in ordinary life, though we want that to be interesting, too. Then there's an inciting incident that changes the life of the central character forever. In this case, it's the capture of the princess, which leads to the message being sent, which leads to, eventually, the death of Luke's aunt and uncle, which leads to his life being changed forever. The goal is set up — he must see that the plans are delivered to the Rebel leaders.

Luke crosses the threshold when he begins his search for a ship to take them to the planet where the Rebel leaders are. In traditional structure, he's gathering his team for action. Once he has his team, he would begin to implement his plan and act 2 would begin. Here he begins to face tests almost immediately when they go to the spaceport and enter the bar. This is stage 6, and the longest of the stages, wherein **the hero encounters tests, gains allies, and faces enemies**.

With Han Solo (Harrison Ford) joining the team, they are ready for their mission. They encounter problems even before they can take off, but Han proves to be a worthy addition to the team and they escape.

Luke begins his training in the ways of the Force, and George Lucas brings Luke's personal journey into focus. He must learn how to use the Force, how to trust the Force, how to let it enter him so that he can direct it for good. Obi-Wan Kenobi, the mentor, teaches him how to use the lightsaber, but also instructs him in the ways of his religion. Luke is on the way to becoming a Jedi Warrior.

Like act 2 in traditional structure, this is the longest section of the film. Many challenges confront them. And they face a turning point. Just when they think they've reached their goal, they find that it has been destroyed. And they're sucked into the Death Star. This is the seventh stage, **where they approach the inmost cave, crossing another threshold**. They are still in act 2 until they escape into the garbage chute. There, Luke is pulled under water by the garbage monster and all appears to be lost. It's **the supreme ordeal of stage eight** and the all-is-lost point of the end of act 2, especially when the walls move in to crush Luke and his team.

We're well into act 3 as they try to flee the ship with the princess. Here, stage 9, **taking possession of the reward**, begins. Luke swings across an abyss with Leia initiating this stage, which is completed when they all (except Obi-Wan Kenobi) escape, carrying the information (in R2-D2) that the Rebels need.

But they are pursued by Imperial fighters on the road back to their (in this case Leia's) ordinary world. This is the beginning of stage 10, **the road back**. The pursuit is more pernicious than it seems. A homing device planted on the ship will lead the Death Star to the planet where the Rebels make their central base.

It's at this point that Han Solo's arc becomes important. He's said he's in it for the money, and he means it. Leia replies that if that's all he loves, that's all he'll get.

The Death Star approaches the Rebel planet, and the Rebels plan the counter-attack. This is going to be the big conflict of the third act, by one way of reckoning. And once they commit to the battle, and Luke is in a fighter on his way to the Death Star, he has crossed the third threshold. In this eleventh stage, Luke will experience **a resurrection and a transformation**. Now this becomes a little confusing in *Star Wars*, because it is Han's character that is resurrected when he comes to Luke's aid, but it's Luke's that is transformed, with the help of Obi-Wan's voice, into a true Jedi Warrior. He lets the Force guide and help him, and thus defeats the enemy. And the Force will be with him always.

The closing sequence is **the return with the elixir** (stage 12) wherein the hero is recognized as the hero by whoever is important to him. His triumphant moment is the return to tranquility and a new life. Here, Luke, Han, and Chewbacca (Peter Mayhew) are recognized as heroes for having saved the Rebel planet. Presumably (and we see that in subsequent episodes), life will be different for all of them now that they've undergone the changes brought about by their journey.

Okay, now let's blow your mind. Did you ever think of *The Wizard of Oz* as a quest movie in the same genre as *Star Wars*? While it fits the seven-point paradigm quite well, it has always bothered me that Dorothy's journey seems to be over when she faces down the Wizard and compels him to give her companions everything they've been striving for. Yet there's still a road home. While discussing this with one of my students, Carol Von Strauss, she pointed out that *The Wizard of Oz* could be seen as a film with a twelve-point structure. She then took the time to lay it out for me. Thanks, Carol.

The Wizard of Oz

Writers: L. Frank Baum (novel *The Wonderful Wizard of Oz*)

Noel Langley, Florence Ryerson, and Edgar Allan Woolf (screenplay)

Act 1

1. **The Ordinary World** — Dorothy (Judy Garland) lives in the bleak dust bowl of Kansas during what seems to be the Depression era.

2. **The Call to Adventure** — With sheriff's order in hand, Miss Gulch (Margaret Hamilton) visits Dorothy's uncle and aunt to take Toto away because he nipped her on the leg.

3. **Refusal of The Call** — Toto escapes from Miss Gulch's basket and returns to Dorothy's bedroom. Dorothy takes Toto and then runs away from home to avoid having Toto taken away from her again.

4. **The Wise Old Man or Woman/Meeting the Mentor** — Dorothy meets Professor Marvel (Frank Morgan) and asks to join him on his travels. He checks his crystal ball for guidance and says he sees a farm woman (Auntie Em, played by Clara Blandick) in distress. Dorothy vows to go back home.

5. **Crossing the First Threshold** — Dorothy arrives home while a twister rages outside. She gets hit in the head with the window, falls on the bed, and then wakes up as the house is spinning in the eye of the cyclone. The house lands in Oz, a vibrant landscape filled with flowers. She meets Glinda the Good Witch (Billie Burke), who tells her to see the Wizard to get back home to Kansas, which is her act 1 goal. The plan is to take the Yellow Brick Road to see the Wizard (Frank Morgan).

Act 2

6. **Tests, Allies, Enemies** — Dorothy meets the Scarecrow (Ray Bolger), who wants a brain; the Tin Man (Jack Haley), who wants a heart; and the Lion (Bert Lahr), who wants courage. One by one, they join Dorothy and Toto on the Yellow Brick Road to Emerald City. They deal with angry apple trees, the sleep spell of the poppy fields, and the Witch's demands for Dorothy to surrender.

7. **The Inmost Cave** — Dorothy and pals arrive at Emerald City to meet the Wizard. The Wizard initially refuses to see Dorothy, but later relents.

Dorothy and pals are terrified of the Wizard. He says he will grant their wishes once they bring back the Wicked Witch's broomstick.

8. **The Supreme Ordeal** — The winged monkeys carry away Dorothy and pals to see the Wicked Witch (Margaret Hamilton). The Witch has plans to kill them and begins by setting the Scarecrow on fire. Dorothy throws a bucket of water to douse the flames and inadvertently kills the Wicked Witch with the water.

9. **Seizing the Sword/Reward** — Dorothy gets to keep her ruby slippers and obtains possession of the broomstick to bring back to the Wizard.

10. **The Road Back** — Dorothy wants to get back home and climbs into a hot air balloon with the Wizard. Toto jumps out of the basket, and Dorothy scrambles after him while the balloon begins its ascent. This is the low point for Dorothy. It looks as if she'll never get home to Kansas again.

Act 3

11. **Resurrection** — Glinda the Good Witch shows up and informs Dorothy that she always had the power to return to Kansas. Glinda didn't tell her initially because she knew that Dorothy wouldn't believe her and had to find it out herself. Glinda tells Dorothy to close her eyes, tap the heels of her ruby slippers three times, and say, "There's no place like home."

12. **Return with the Elixir** — Dorothy wakes up in her bed murmuring the magic words. She realizes that everything was a dream and tells the people around her bed (Auntie Em, Uncle Henry [Charley Grapewin], Zeke [Bert Lahr], Hunk [Ray Bolger], and Hickory [Jack Haley]) about her adventures. She tells everyone she loves them and emphatically states that she'll never leave because there is no place like home. (That's the elixir, the secret to life.)

Of course, this is a structure Carol superimposed on the film. It's unlikely that the writers were aware of Campbell's mythic structure, just as folk storytellers throughout the centuries were unaware of the structure they were unconsciously using. But it was there, in varying degrees, in thousands of stories in hundreds of cultures. It may be a valuable structure for you to employ.

Just for good luck, let's summarize the structure:

There are twelve steps that roughly fit into the traditional three-act structure.

Act 1

1. Heroes are introduced in The Ordinary World, where ...
2. They receive The Call to Adventure.
3. They are Reluctant at first or Refuse the Call, but ...
4. Are encouraged by a Mentor to ...
5. Cross the first threshold and enter the Special World, where ...

Act 2

6. They encounter Tests, Allies, and Enemies.
7. They Approach the Inmost Cave, crossing the second threshold ...
8. Where they endure The Supreme Ordeal (death and rebirth — and pick something up from the cave).
9. They take possession of their Reward (seizing the sword) and ...
10. Are pursued on The Road Back to the Ordinary World.

Act 3

11. They cross the third threshold, experience a Resurrection, and are transformed by the experience (second life-and-death moment — this mirrors the supreme ordeal).
12. They Return with the Elixir, a boon or treasure to benefit the Ordinary World.

Is it better to look at a film, or construct a film, this way, or is the traditional three-act play a more meaningful method of analysis? That depends entirely on the film. You probably could look at any of the *Superman* or *Batman* films in this way and find the twelve points. On the other hand, it probably wouldn't work for *Animal House* or even *A Beautiful Mind*. It's a form that works best for heroic action films. But if it's used to support the story in that type of film, it can lend the resonance of myth that can only strengthen the impact of the movie.

To Do

Can you reconceive your film as a mythic quest with the twelve steps? Write it briefly here. Does it make more sense to structure your film this way or in the traditional seven points?

THE POWERFUL PROTAGONIST

"Character is the fundamental material we are forced to work with, so we must know character as thoroughly as possible."

— Lajos Egri, *The Art of Dramatic Writing*

Movies are not abstractions like modern art. They are based on people — their interactions, their responses to conflict, their emotions. The building blocks of movies are characters: interesting, vital, dynamic, funny, weird, scary, stupid, bizarre characters. And every movie is the story of one person's emotional (and often physical) journey. Notice I said "one person's."

Students frequently ask me if there can be more than one central character. What about *Butch Cassidy and the Sundance Kid*? What about *Thelma & Louise*? The answer is that these are buddy pictures, but there still is one buddy who is dominant, around whom the story revolves. In *Butch* it's Butch. In *Thelma & Louise*, it's Thelma (does placement in the title give you a hint?). But what about ensemble movies? I usually ask, "Like which ensemble movies?" A sharp class will come up with one — *The Big Chill*. A really sharp class will add another — *The Secaucus Seven*. And maybe *The Breakfast Club*. (*Ocean's Eleven* isn't.) Then you're done. And even if you could come up with more, they would still be the exception. And even though there are no rules, audiences find it confusing to deal with more than one central character. And since a movie is defined by the journey of one character, it's important to figure out who the central character is before you go any further.

That's why I'm going to tell you about the single most important thing you must know about your central character, your protagonist: "What does he want?" Though this may change later to "What does he need?" it is the driving force of the movie. It defines your character. It motivates the action. Everything that happens in the movie happens because your central character is pursuing a goal. That's what pushes the action. That's what causes the changes. That's what tells us who the character is. So, do you have the right protagonist for your movie, and do you know what he wants?

Matching Character to Premise

The first thing we have to ask before reviewing our characters is, what is this movie about? What is its premise? Then we can make sure our central character proves this premise. By premise, I'm talking about Egri's definition of premise: the central thesis of the movie, what you are setting out to prove. It could be "great love defies even death," as it is in *Titanic* (and *Romeo and Juliet*). It could be "greed destroys the soul," as it is in *The Treasure of the Sierra Madre* (and in *The Merchant of Venice*).

Characters Come Out of Premise. Premise Comes from Characters.

Premise is the underlying message that you're trying to sneak into your movie. You really do want to say something as well as entertain, don't you? Executives will cite Samuel Goldwyn's line, "If you want to send a message, use Western Union," but, really, if a film is not about something, it's not going to be worth watching. Even the simplest films have a premise. (You might call it a theme, an idea, a subject, whatever term you want. Egri calls it premise.)

The premise is usually expressed in one line and doesn't contain the words *is* or *are* (which merely state definitions). Here are some premises from contemporary films: "Underestimating nature leads to disaster" for *The Perfect Storm*. "Right conquers tyranny" for *The Patriot*. "Cooperation and hope will free you from bondage" from *Chicken Run*. Yes, *Chicken Run*. "With great power comes great responsibility" from *Spider-Man*.

Before we go any further in the exploration of character, think about what you are really trying to say with your story. I'm not talking about a one-line summary of the action. I'm talking about the message that underlies everything, the deepest core of the movie.

To Do

Write your premise here. Do not use the words *is* or *are*. Do not tell the story, only the idea of the truth you want to prove.

Matching the Characters to the Premise

Once you have an idea what your movie is about, you must make sure that your characters will help you prove your premise. When you first write your movie, you can find the characters and then look for a premise. It's harder to do it that way. I've done it, and so have lots of other people. But if you know what your characters have to achieve ahead of time, it makes it easier to find the kind of characters you need. But you already have your characters, so let's make sure they're a good match.

For example, in *Romeo and Juliet*, if Romeo had been thoughtful and cautious, say, like Hamlet, the story would have gone nowhere. The premise of "great love defies even death" would never have been proven with Hamlet as the central character. If George Clooney's character, Captain Billy Tyne, had been cautious, there would have been no story in *The Perfect Storm*.

The personalities of these characters drove these stories. Their actions proved the premises. And only these characters would have worked.

Maybe you're thinking that these characters created these plots, and you would be right. Certainly without the Clooney character, there is no plot, just a big storm. Without the Mel Gibson character's background, without his love for his family, without his slip into a killing frenzy, there would be no *The Patriot*. Without Alvy Singer's nebbish personality and quirky sense of humor, there would be no *Annie Hall*. What would *Bill and Ted's Excellent Adventure* be without Bill and Ted? *Groundhog Day* without the cynical Phil Connors?

Tootsie without the grating, difficult-to-work-with Michael Dorsey? *Avatar* without physically and psychologically impaired Jake Sully?

So, does your character help prove your premise? Is he a good match?

Character Construction

Let's find out who your character is to make sure he's the right one for your premise. If he isn't, we can adjust him … or the premise. How do we find out? By deconstructing him. You have a person in mind, but can the audience see him clearly? They will if you know your character.

Lajos Egri, in *The Art of Dramatic Writing*, says there are three components to every character: the physiological, the sociological, and the psychological. In other words, what they look like physically, where they come from and what their circumstances are now, and what their thought processes and emotions are. It's also good to include their goals and the flaws or quirks that set them apart. For example, let's look at the Mel Gibson character, Benjamin Martin, in *The Patriot*, written by Robert Rodat:

Mel Gibson, The Patriot, *written by Robert Rodat, directed by Roland Emmerich (Columbia Pictures, 2000).*

The Ghost, Benjamin Martin

Physiology: Forties. Dark hair. Rugged looking. In good shape.

Sociology: Plantation owner, but does not own slaves. Widower. Father of six. Former army captain. Legislator. Famous.

Psychology: Suffers from post-traumatic stress as a result of the French and Indian War. Afraid that sins would revisit him. (And they do.) Slow to anger, but a mighty temper. Failed furniture maker, but doesn't give up. Sentimental. Soft-spoken. Pacifist until forced. Family, freedom, and frenzy would be an accurate short list of his concerns.

Flaw that he must overcome: His bloodlust.

Goal: To stay out of war. To rescue son. To win war.

Or let's look at George Bailey, from *It's a Wonderful Life*, screenplay by Frances Goodrich, Albert Hackett, and Frank Capra; additional scenes by Jo Swerling; based on a story by Phillip Van Doren Stern:

<u>George Bailey</u>

Physiology: Starts as a child. Loses hearing (after saving brother). Grows tall and slender.

Sociology: Middle-class, intact family. Father is the head of a savings and loan (George goes to his office). Has a maid. Has a younger brother whom he saves. Works in a drugstore as a child, takes over father's business. People like him (Mary whispers into his ear; the other girl likes him, too). Lives in a small town. Never gets to college or to travel.

Psychology: Interested in travel, adventure. Willing to risk life to save others. Compassionate. Speaks his mind. Happy and not afraid to show it. Loves his father. Loyal. Sincere. Patriotic.

Flaw: Has a temper.

Goal: To do something big and important.

Even characters in animated films can be created in this way. Did you see *Ratatouille*? A classic Pixar film, written and directed by Brad Bird, story by Jan Pinkava, Jim Capobianco, and Brad Bird, it features a rat in the central role. One of the great accomplishments of the film, and there are many, is that they make a rat, Remy, a sympathetic character with a minimum of exposition.

Remy, voiced by Patton Oswalt, Ratatouille, *written and directed by Brad Bird, story by Jan Pinkava, Jim Capobianco, and Brad Bird (Pixar, 2007).*

<u>Remy</u>

Physiology: He appears to be a little smaller than the other rats, especially his brother. He could be an adolescent — we're not sure — but he is certainly a rat. Physiologically, he stands out because he can walk on his hind legs like a human. He does this so his hands are free.

Sociology: He belongs to an extended rat family. His mother is never mentioned, but his father is prominent, as is his brother, who eventually leads him into trouble. He lives with the family in the attic of a farmhouse, but spends most of his time on a trash pile with the others eating. His father is the leader of the whole extended family of rats. He's never lived anywhere else.

Psychology: He has discovered the miracle of combining flavors and exalts in it. He has a highly sensitive nose, which his father uses as a test for poison in their food, but which he prefers to use to smell ingredients and then taste the food that he prepares from them. He is enthralled by Chef Gusteau and wants to be a cook.

Flaw: Willing to steal, if necessary, in order to achieve his goals.

Goal: To become a chef.

The more you know about your central character, the better you will write about him. As you rewrite, you may be putting your character into new situations with new people, and you'll need to know who he is in order to write his behavior and dialogue and to make him consistent throughout the story. Also, when the time comes to rewrite his dialogue, you'll be more conversant with who your protagonist is and so his speech and actions will flow more freely from your fingertips.

To Do

Write a profile of your central character.
Name:
Physiology: (including age)
Sociology:
Psychology:
Goal:
Personality Flaw That Hinders Him:

Motivation

The clearer your picture of your character, the clearer you'll be able to express him in print and the better you will be able to motivate his actions. Knowing where he comes from, both physically and mentally, will tell you where he's going. Now he has reasons to do things, not just for the convenience of the story, but organically. What your character does in response to the challenges in your story is who your character is. John Sacret Young, co-creator of *China Beach* and writer of *Testament* and *Romero*, says, "Problems come up when you don't know the character well enough."

Consistency

The next thing to check for is consistency. Is your character consistent in his responses throughout your script, or does he sometimes do things that are out of character? Sure, he can do surprising things, so long as they make sense within the character that you have constructed. Alvy Singer wouldn't lift weights in his spare time. Michael Dorsey wouldn't take an insult calmly. Hannibal Lecter wouldn't use bad grammar — except for effect.

To Do

Review your script and make sure your central character acts consistently with the personality you've given him. Ensure that each action and each word make sense for the character's physiology, sociology, and psychology.

Making Your Character Watchable

You know in the first five minutes whether you like a movie or not. A major part of that is how you feel towards the central character. In most Hollywood movies, that means either we like him or he's so intensely interesting that he compels our attention. Think about it. How many films are successful that have unredeemed jerks as their central character? Sure, you can name a couple of exceptions — try *Scarface* or even *The Godfather II*. But they are the exceptions, and they feature intensely interesting people. But even in movies in which the protagonist starts out as a jerk, he usually ends up as something else. Think of Jim Carrey's character, Fletcher Reede, in *Liar Liar*, written by Paul Guay and Stephen Mazur. Even though he's despicable in many ways at the beginning of the story, there's something we like about him — he loves his son and he's funny. (It helps that Mazur is a world-class wisecracker.)

In other movies it can be the character's sense of humor, looks, or vulnerability that wins us over. Most of all, though, it's their flaws and quirks that make us identify with the protagonist. Flaws make a character more interesting. The good guy has some bad qualities. That makes him human. Approachable. Believable. Part of his conflict is fighting those qualities.

Nicholas Kazan, writer of *Frances*, *Reversal of Fortune*, and *Bicentennial Man*, among others, puts it this way: The character doesn't have to be likable, just compelling. Readers and viewers have to be able to see themselves as that person. "As long as he is emotionally true," Kazan says, "then you're on the ride."

To Do

What makes your character watchable? Notice, I didn't say likable. Write that here in one sentence or less:

_____

_____

If you don't have a good answer for that, go back and rethink your character sketch. Whatever you come up with, you will have to incorporate into the sketch and then into the script.

The Goal

This is the single most important thing you must know about your protagonist. If a character has no goal, then she's passive, and the world works on her. She's nobody. She's rolling with the punches. She's not active. She's not central. She's not pushing the action; she's being pulled by it. The word *protagonist* can be defined in several ways — one, in the theatrical way meaning the leading character or hero. But it can also be defined as a person who champions a cause. Your leading character must champion a cause, even if it's her own. She *must* have a goal.

But she doesn't usually have one at the beginning of your movie. She doesn't know what she wants, not until something happens to her at the inciting incident, which will compel her to develop a goal. By the end of act 1, though, she will know what that goal is, and she'll have a plan to pursue it. Events may occur in the middle of act 2 that force her to change that goal or to realize that her inner need is a more important goal, but the pursuit of a goal will be foremost in her mind throughout the film.

Katniss' goal in *The Hunger Games* is to save her sister, which then changes to survival. Schatze Page's (Lauren Bacall) goal in *How to Marry a Millionaire* is, cynically, to marry a millionaire, but, in the end, it changes to marrying for love. Thelma's goal at the end of act 1 of *Thelma & Louise* is to flee to Mexico, but it morphs into taking charge of her own life.

Marilyn Monroe, Betty Grable, Lauren Bacall, How to Marry a Millionaire, *written by Nunnally Johnson, based on the play by Zoe Akins, Dale Eunson, and Katherine Albert, directed by Jean Negulesco (20th Century Fox, 1953).*

These goals drive these women throughout their journeys. They inform every single scene. They force the stories forward. Without goals, there is no story. Without story, you end up with something like Terrence Malick's *The Tree of Life* — something beautiful to look at, but not compelling (and a box-office failure).

As a writer, you must know what the goal is and what that goal changes to. You must ensure that she's driving towards that goal in every scene. That's what pushes her.

To Do

What is the apparent goal of your protagonist? What does that goal change to at the midpoint? (In other words, what does she *really* want and need?)

The Flaw

But there's something that prevents your hero from reaching that goal. Yes, there's an antagonist, be it Mother Nature as in *The Perfect Storm* or the federal marshal as in *The Fugitive*. More on that later. But there's another very powerful force that hinders his progress towards his goal, one that he must overcome in order to reach it, and that's his personality flaw.

Developing the Flaw

Nobody's perfect. You've heard that said a million times. You've even used it as an excuse yourself. But you know it to be true. You've never met a perfect individual, not even your significant other. Not even your perfect child. Not even, dare I say this, the president. Not even Superman. Sure, Superman has a physical weakness — he's allergic to kryptonite. But physical flaws don't count. We're talking about personality, even psychological, flaws. Superman never shows his true self. He leads a double life. He finds it hard to connect with people. He's flawed. In short, Superman is human, too.

People will not want to watch your story if your characters aren't human, especially your central character. And to be human, he must be flawed. Shy. Arrogant. Emotionally unavailable. Impetuous. Lacking in confidence. Lacking in social graces. Lacking in maturity. And any one of these or a hundred other flaws can make your protagonist's journey difficult. The flaw is the thing inside himself that your protagonist must overcome in order to defeat the thing outside himself that stands between him and his goal. As Anderson says, "Filling out imperfect people is easier than making a perfect character interesting."

Ryan Bingham (George Clooney) in *Up in the Air* refuses to connect emotionally with the people he fires (or anyone else) — until he does and becomes vulnerable. Thelma doesn't stand up or think for herself — until she does. Philippe (François Cluzet) in *The Intouchables* (yes, I'm using a French film as an example because it is constructed very much like a Hollywood film), is afraid to go outside of his comfort zone until he does and learns that there still can be joy in his life.

So, again, go to your sketch. Think about the psychological traits your character has. Know what your character's baggage is. What is his loss? Think of the flaws he has. Which one is standing between him and his goal? Which one do you need to emphasize from the very first time we see the protagonist so we know what the issue is that he faces? That's the second most important thing you must know about your character. It's the one that gets in the way of the first most important thing (the goal).

To Do

What in your central character's persona (anger, insecurity, arrogance, greed, inability to connect or commit, selfishness, etc.) is preventing him from reaching his goal? How does this stop him?

Revealing Character through Action

How many times have you heard people who talk about writing say, "Action is character?" What does that mean? It's simple. We define people by what they do (and what they say). Just telling us that a person is charismatic doesn't help in a movie, but showing us how that person uses his magnetism to influence people does (John Wayne in *Fort Apache* or a score of other movies). You can't tell your audience that a character is shy; you must show him in a situation where his actions tell us he is shy (Superman meeting Lois Lane). As a last resort, you can have people talk about him and tell each other he's shy, but nothing works like showing him in a situation where he hides from someone he's afraid to meet or is silent when someone flirts with him. Action is character. A person *is* what he does.

Dirty Harry puts a gun to a man's head and threatens him. Superman leaps tall buildings. Dorothy runs away from the farm and her problems. Luke runs away from his farm to save the universe. Thelma packs a gun, handling it gingerly, then later uses the gun to hold up a convenience store. Each action tells us something about the character at that stage of his or her development. What these characters do is what they are.

To Do

Write one-line descriptions of three scenes in which your character does something to show who he or she is. If you don't have these scenes yet, create them.

1. _____

2. _____

3. _____

Other Ways to Reveal Character

Something as simple as wardrobe can reveal character. In *Erin Brockovich*, the way Erin is dressed tells us a lot about the character. Clearly set up by Susannah Grant, with an assist by Richard LaGravenese (and based on the real person), Erin is flamboyant and not at all afraid to show her body. And another notable trait follows suit — she uses flamboyant language as well, and she's not afraid to speak her mind. She is a character to remember.

It could be the character's surroundings as well as wardrobe. We see the difference between Felix and Oscar in Neil Simon's *The Odd Couple* through their rooms — one neat, the other messy. Phillip Vandamm (James Mason) in *North by Northwest* is defined by his living quarters — neat, angular, cold. Tony Stark (Robert Downey Jr.) in *The Avengers* lives on the top floor of a modern skyscraper in technical and creature luxury. He is where he lives.

Julia Roberts, Erin Brockovich, *written by Susannah Grant, directed by Steven Soderbergh (Jersey Films, 2000).*

Dialogue

What a character says and how she says it is important. It's what made the film *Erin Brockovich* rise above a boring legal proceeding. What she says is who she is. One of the first things that tells you about a character is what that character sounds like. Her level of education, her place of origin, her state of mind are all reflected in her speech. Think of *Forrest Gump.* Think of *A Coal Miner's Daughter.* Captain Kirk in *Star Trek* sounds different than Mr. Spock, who sounds very different than Spike Lee in *She's Gotta Have It* or Easy Rollins in *Devil with a Blue Dress,* or Jimmy Smits in *Mi Familia.*

The Arc de Character

If you've spent any time at all in Hollywood — virtual or real — you've heard the term *character arc.* This is an essential term of art that simply means, "How does your character change?" As discussed earlier, your character must have a flaw. The journey to correct that flaw is the character arc. It's what effect the trials and tribulations of the story have on the character of the character. In other words, how does what happens affect our protagonist? How does he change from a pompous, self-centered cynic, like the

Bill Murray character in Danny Rubin's *Groundhog Day* (rewrite by Harold Ramis), to the caring, loving man at the end, capable of true despair and ultimately true happiness? There's the arc — from A to Z, but with lots of stops along the way. By the way, rent *Groundhog Day* for a look at a truly different way to study a character using the same events over and over but playing for a different effect each time.

Let's look at the protagonist of another modern classic, Thelma (Geena Davis), of *Thelma & Louise*. When we first meet Thelma, she's a suburban housewife seemingly incapable of making a decision without consulting her husband. Her life is out of her control. She's a virtual slave. She has no ambition of her own.

Then, step by step, she takes control of her life, first by going away with Louise (Susan Sarandon), then by deciding to really have fun at the roadhouse. But things spin out of control, and she doesn't know how to handle herself until the midpoint when she is emancipated sexually by J.D. (Brad Pitt). Somehow, now she has the power to take her life in her own hands, to become the driver of the story when Louise is in a deep funk, and even to enter into a new vocation — convenience store robber.

In the end, surrounded by men, she chooses a death of freedom and self-determination. It may be a pessimistic ending, but at least it's one she chooses, finally the mistress of her own destiny. She has changed drastically.

So, does your character change? Did she go from a self-effacing coward to a self-confident hero? The change doesn't have to be that grandiose, but it must be noticeable. And the progress of this C story must also have its own structure — at least a beginning, a middle, and an end. And we know, from our discussion above, that your protagonist must overcome her flaw in order to prevail in the final challenge, so we can see that the seven points of the character-arc story again fall in line with the seven points of the central story. When you go through your script focusing on just the character, make sure that his or her arc has enough screen time to be essential to the story and that its major points are in line with the goal-driven A story.

It's a lot to remember. Feel free to reread this chapter at any time in the process. The emotional story and the character arc are intimately entwined with the A story and are key to giving life to your protagonist.

To Do

Put your emotional story's seven points next to your character arc's seven points and make sure there's a relationship.

Jim Carrey, The Cable Guy, *written by Lou Holtz Jr., directed by Ben Stiller (Columbia Pictures, 1996).*

Making Sure Your Protagonist Is All You Want Him to Be

One of the key ways to get your script from being 110 pages of paper with words on them to becoming 10,000 feet of celluloid running through a projector (or a file streamed to a theater) is to attach a star to it. And the only way to do that is to write a part that the star will want to play. That could mean different things for different stars. A comedy specialist, say, Jim Carrey, might want to play a serious role, as in *The Cable Guy*. A chameleon like Meryl Streep might want to play an action role as in *The River Wild*. A child star like Macaulay Culkin might want to show he's an adult, as he does in *Sex and Breakfast*. It may just be a showy role, such as the one Jack Nicholson played in *As Good as It Gets*. Or it may be a very earnest and sympathetic figure like the one Will Smith played in *The Pursuit of Happyness*. In any case, you must offer the actors a role to sink their teeth into, something that will enhance their career, make them look good, or, at least, look like a good actor. How do you do that? By making the protagonist all you want him to be.

To Do

I use this checklist in my classes to make sure my students have fully developed their protagonists. Before you rewrite your central character, complete this list to help give direction to your rewrite.

- No indecisive, do-nothing characters. (They can be indecisive as a character flaw, but it must be something they overcome in order to reach their goal.)

- No passive characters (again, passivity may be a flaw they overcome, but that means by taking action). Your protagonist must push the action. The action can't all just "happen" to him. He drives the story.

- Does your protagonist have a passion or obsession that drives him or her?

- Is he seeking something?

- Does the character speak in his own way?

- Nobody is without flaws.

- Nobody is without idiosyncrasies.

- Your protagonist must have a sense of humor.

- We must know the protagonist's surroundings, job, and home.

- Characters grow — they have a desire for change. Do yours?

- Characters prove your premise.

- Know all three components of their makeup and test them in action.

Now What?

- Now you have a thorough understanding of who your character is, what he wants, how he would act in any particular situation, and how he changes.

- Now, what's he up against?

But, first, it's time for a little break. Take a writing session off and look at a movie in the same genre as the one you're working on. Don't take notes. Just let it settle in. Enjoy it. Imagine that you wrote it. Nice, huh?

THE CENTRAL
EMOTIONAL RELATIONSHIP

We watch movies because of the people in the movies. Even movies loaded with special effects have to have people in them, people about whom we care. And it's not just about the people; it's about the people relating to other people. To be more precise, it's about your central character relating to another person.

In every movie, even in action movies, there has to be a central emotional relationship (CER). This is one way to humanize your protagonist. It's a way to show his emotional journey as well as his "story" journey (the one focused on his goal). It's a way to relate to the protagonist on a human level and to root for him. It's a way to ground the story in an emotional reality that everyone can understand.

It doesn't have to be a romantic relationship. It can be a buddy relationship as in *Thelma & Louise*. It can be a stand-in father/daughter relationship as in *Million Dollar Baby*. It can be a mentor/student relationship as in *Star Wars*. The point is, there must be an emotional relationship at the core of your movie to give it heart.

This emotional relationship can take two forms. Either it is an emotional relationship that must be established or one that must be repaired. Sometimes, this relationship is the center of the movie, as in a romantic comedy such as *The Philadelphia Story* or *You've Got Mail*. (So it, in fact, becomes the A story, while the plot becomes the B story.) Sometimes the relationship is the B story and serves to support the A story, as in *Armageddon* or *Avatar*. Sometimes it's barely there, as in *The Avengers*, but it's there.

Does your story have a key emotional relationship? If it doesn't, now's the time to create one or beef one up. And the emotional relationship should, like your movie, have a beginning, a middle, and an end. As a matter of fact, it should follow the same seven-point paradigm that your A story follows (see chapter 1). Often, the story points for your emotional story correspond to the A story points, but not always. They'll be close, though, so when you restructure according to chapter 1, keep that in mind. For now, just focus on the emotional story itself.

Helen Hunt and John Hawkes, The Sessions, *written and directed by Ben Lewin (Such Much Films and Fox Searchlight, 2012).*

Let's look at two films with unusual central emotional relationships. The first, a small picture that was a big hit at Sundance, was written and directed by Ben Lewin. Originally called *The Surrogate, The Sessions* is about Mark O'Brien, who has lived in an iron lung since contracting polio at age six, and, at age thirty-eight, decides he wants to lose his virginity. A tremendously poignant film starring John Hawkes, Helen Hunt, and William Macy, the central emotional relationship naturally concerns Mark's (Hawkes) relationship with Cheryl Cohen Greene (Hunt), the surrogate with whom he develops a sexual relationship. Though it could have possibly turned into a love story, it doesn't, but they have a very special relationship. And, while it's very important to the A story, it is not the A story — achieving a life with sexual pleasure and meaning is.

In *Argo*, written by Chris Terrio based on an article by Joshuah Bearman, Tony Mendez (played by Ben Affleck) has a rather tenuous relationship with his wife, from whom he's taking a break, and his son, with whom he communicates with some regularity. But neither of these is the central emotional relationship that must be created or mended. If they were, he would do something to repair them. But he does nothing.

So what is the CER in this film? It's with the six Americans hiding in the residence of the Canadian ambassador to Iran, whom he must convince to trust him so he can extricate them from the country. The film's A story is the process by which he is recruited, creates a plan, enters the country, and prepares the group to escape. The B story is his developing a relationship with the group — not any specific individual — so that they trust him to accomplish his mission. It's a gripping story which has you on the edge of your seat for both reasons — will he convince them to go along with him, and will he be successful in shepherding them out of Tehran? The A and the B story work together to provide the suspense, aided by the editing, which is also superb.

To Do

Write out the seven points of your B story on a separate piece of paper. Compare them side by side with the A story. Do they coincide in time in terms of your film? It's okay if they don't, but it's best if they're close. Each lends power to the other. If you can't find the seven points of your central-emotional-relationship story, then it probably isn't well enough developed. It needs more. Relationships in real life have ups and downs. They do in movies, too. Flesh out this relationship and you'll add involvement in the story that you didn't have before.

THE WORTHY ANTAGONIST

If there is no barrier for your protagonist, he will achieve his goal immediately. There is no conflict, so there is no story. (Remember the definition of story.) While this may occasionally happen in real life, it is rare that someone achieves a goal without some difficulty. The more difficulty, the sweeter the victory and the more interesting a story to tell.

The same applies to movie life. If there is nothing to overcome, there is no story. The movie's over before it has a chance to start. So there must be something or someone in opposition, something or someone that makes it hard, almost impossible, for your protagonist to reach his goal. Without struggle there is no story, and the bigger the struggle, the better the story.

So your protagonist must have opposition. And the clearest way to put roadblocks in front of your central character is to put another person in the way. There are some exceptions — nature is antagonist enough for *The Perfect Storm* or *Volcano*. In a war movie, it's the enemy, sometimes personified, but often not.

What is an antagonist? It's a person whose goals are in conflict with the protagonist's. It could be a business competitor, a competitor in love, a criminal (if your protagonist is a detective), a detective (if your protagonist is a criminal), anyone who has a reason to be in the way of the protagonist's goal and actively exercises it.

The antagonist is the second most important person in your film. He has to be a worthy opponent because he must provide the most important barrier to the protagonist's drive toward his goal. If he is too weak, then the fight is too small. He must be stronger than the protagonist, better, faster, smarter, more handsome (in a romantic comedy, at least). His opposition must force the protagonist to rise above himself to reach his goal. He must be a worthy foe. If he's not, there is no movie.

Adding Depth

If your antagonist is a human being, he must have humane qualities to avoid being two-dimensional and predictable. A purely evil protagonist is not interesting. Even a man who runs a concentration camp, exterminating people all day long, may return to a loving wife, children, and a dog. A murderer may have a weakness for sweets. A business rival may harbor a secret passion for music — or S&M. This adds depth to the characterization as well as reality. Even Hitler was reputedly kind to his secretary, and there is footage of him playing with his dogs. It makes his evil all the more chilling.

Just as your protagonist must have a flaw, your antagonist must have a good quality, one the audience can identify as human.

I'm not saying, either, that your antagonist has to be evil. In a romantic comedy, he shouldn't be. He should be a serious possibility when it comes to being a potential love object (see *Tin Cup* or *His Girl Friday*). In a sports movie, he's the opposition, though often less morally worthy of the goal than the protagonist, but he is not pure evil (*Bad News Bears*, *Rocky*). That's too easy. Yes, we still must have a reason to consider him less worthy of winning, so he must have some evil characteristics. But he is a human being with all the wants and needs of a human being.

To Do

How do you draw a character like this? The same way you develop the protagonist. Ask yourself: Do you know this character as well as you know your protagonist? Before you rewrite his role in your script, take the time now to write a character study in the same way you did for your protagonist. This time, pay special attention to elements that may explain why he went down the path to evil, if that's the kind of antagonist you have, or why he thinks he's fighting for what's his or what is right, according to him. Also, be careful to include a humanizing trait. Nobody is completely evil. Nobody is completely good. To be believable, your antagonist must ring true as a person.

Revealing the Antagonist

Character is action. Action is character. When you read through your script (and you should read it through several times before undertaking your rewrite), look for places to show the character of your antagonist. Look for places to show how he interacts with people on a daily basis, how he interacts with his confederates or his family. Look for places to show his human side. And, especially, look for places to show his strengths and weaknesses and, if necessary, his evil.

Just as the protagonist has a voice, so should the antagonist, assuming your antagonist is a person. Things to check for in the antagonist's dialogue: Is he too arch (over-the-top) evil? Does he sound human, or is he just a writer's two-dimensional conceit to move the story along?

Once you've read this character's dialogue completely through, compare and contrast his words with the protagonist's words. Make sure they're not speaking with the same voice. Their rhythms of speech should be distinct, their vocabularies in contrast. Ensure that how they say something is as important as what they say.

For an excellent example of contrasting manners of speech and a worthy opponent, look at Hans Gruber, the character played by Alan Rickman in *Die Hard* (screenplay by Jeb Stuart based on the novel by Roderick Thorp). Here is an antagonist whose speech demonstrates his erudition and ruthlessness. He is able, in a critical moment, to imitate the speech of an American executive, thus showing his cunning. His manner of talking is a fundamental element of his character, just as fundamental as John McClane's (Bruce Willis) blue-collar, wisecracking, no-nonsense speech.

Alan Rickman, Die Hard, *written by Jeb Stuart and Steven E. de Souza, based on the novel by Roderick Thorp, directed by John McTiernan (20th Century Fox, 1988).*

But it isn't only his speech that he uses to deceive McClane; it is his cowering manner. He "acts" like the victim to perfection, trying to gain McClane's confidence. Eventually, McClane gives him a pistol. Once he has his hands on the pistol, his whole demeanor changes, and he becomes Hans again. There's another reversal when he discovers that the pistol is not loaded and that he hadn't fooled McClane after all. And yet another reversal when other members of his gang burst out of the elevator.

Definitely a worthy foe — ruthless, cunning, quick-witted, multilingual. Try and stop him! McClane finally does, but he pays a price. It isn't easy, but the journey is worth it.

To Do

Write one line saying what your antagonist wants.

The Story from the Antagonist's Point of View

Now consider the seven points from the antagonist's point of view. Some of these points may not appear in your screenplay. We don't really need to know the ordinary life of your antagonist, but you, as the writer, do. Keep in mind that 1) the antagonist also has a goal or goals and they could change, and 2) his seven points are sometimes the opposite of the protagonist's points.

For example, the low point for the protagonist is actually the *high point* for the antagonist. And the antagonist will eventually lose in the final challenge. Also, we don't really need to know what happens to him in the return to the now-changed-forever normal life.

Let's look at *Les Misérables* for a classic antagonist with specific goals. In this film, adapted from the stage musical adapted from Victor Hugo's immense novel, screenplay by William Nicholson with many stage writing credits, Jean Valjean (Hugh Jackman) is the protagonist. His goals are simple: at first, to live a free life in the service of God. Then he takes on the care of Cosette (Amanda Seyfried), the daughter of one of his workers. His goal is to raise her as he promised her mother.

But Javert (Russell Crowe), the antagonist, has a competing goal — to return Jean Valjean, prisoner 24601 to justice. As such, he gets in the way of Jean Valjean's goals, no matter what alias he has taken on. In the end, in what may be described as Jean Valjean's final challenge, Javert is vanquished by Valjean's goodness and the memory of how Valjean saved him from the rebels. He can't handle the contradictions and throws himself off a bridge, unbeknownst to Valjean.

In *Inglourious Basterds*, Quentin Tarantino sets up a villain, Colonel Hans Landa (Christoph Waltz), whose goal is to track down hidden Jews. He pursues his goal while Lieutenant Aldo Raine (Brad Pitt) pursues his — the tracking down and killing of as many Nazis as possible. Obviously, their goals are in conflict. It could be argued that the real protagonist of the movie is Shosanna Dreyfus (Mélanie Laurent), who has been on the run from Landa since he killed her family. In the end, her goal is to murder as many Nazis as possible in a suicidal conflagration. She succeeds with the help of Raine.

The point is, a clear-cut antagonist with specific goals of his or her own creates a dynamic that delivers gripping drama.

ENSURING DYNAMIC SCENES
AND SEQUENCES

Only one type of scene should be in your movie: a scene that moves the story forward and illuminates character. If a scene doesn't do one or both of these chores, then that scene doesn't belong in your screenplay. Once your scene passes that litmus test, what else do you need to know about your scene to make sure it's a good one?

Just as a good screenplay has a solid foundation in its structure, so does a scene. A scene has a beginning, a middle, and an end. It actually has all the seven points that a screenplay has; you just don't always see all the parts. Good writers come in as late as possible in the scripted scene and leave as soon as their point is made, but the scene as a whole has taken place on or off camera.

Look at *Shakespeare in Love*, written by Marc Norman and Tom Stoppard, one of the best screenplays of the last twenty-five years or so. A scene that exemplifies the seven-point structure comes near the middle of the story, when Viola, dressed as Thomas, returns to her home.

The ordinary life of the scene starts with a quick shot of her reading Shakespeare's love note to Viola and continues with Essex ranting in her chambers. When she enters as Viola, there is some small talk.

The inciting incident of the scene is when Essex announces that he has entered into a contract with her father for her hand in marriage. At this stage, Viola is still the protagonist of the scene, but that changes when she says she doesn't want the marriage to happen. Now it's Essex's turn to be the protagonist. He has a goal. He has come for something — to state his intentions to marry her and take her to Virginia. End of act 1 of the scene.

The turning point of the scene is when he grabs and kisses her. She slaps him, turning the scene around and changing his attitude from solicitous (as solicitous as he can be, at least) to forceful and demanding. This is the low point for Essex. But he rebounds, and, for what is the low point for Viola, he tells her how it's going to be with him in the Americas.

Gwyneth Paltrow and Colin Firth, Shakespeare in Love, *written by Marc Norman and Tom Stoppard, directed by John Madden (Universal Pictures and Miramax Films, 1998).*

In the final challenge, he overcomes her objections by telling her that the queen and her father have consented, meaning there's no way out. She capitulates. He has reached his goal.

There is no real return to normal life because the point has been made, time to move on. It's quite common to skip the first and last points in a scene, as they are often understood by the actions before and after them, and they do not need to be explained. Get in late and get out early.

Just as there are barriers (conflict) that the protagonist must overcome throughout the film, so, too, there are smaller conflicts in each scene. In the beginning of a scene, somebody wants something. Somebody else either tries to prevent him from getting that or wants something in opposition. The scene, then, is about the struggle. Learning what each one (or more) wants is the beginning of the scene. The struggle to get it is the middle. One or the other wins the struggle. That's the end of the scene. Somebody's got to win; somebody's got to lose. Even in a comedy. Especially in a comedy.

The central characteristic, the one element that every scene needs, is conflict. If there is no conflict, there is no scene. Let me say that again, as this is one of the biggest flaws in new writers' screenplays: IF THERE IS NO CONFLICT, THERE IS NO SCENE. There must be conflict or the scene does not move the story, is not part of the story, is simply an *event*. Life is full of events. Movies are not. Movies are stories, the major component part of which is the scene that contains conflict.

To be perfectly clear: A wedding is an event. A wedding interrupted by an ex-wife with a gun who fires it in the air before the vows are said is the start of a story. Going out to eat with the intention of proposing to your fiancée, then doing it, and getting a yes is an event. Going out to eat with the intention of proposing to your fiancée, losing the ring in the bathroom while practicing the proposal, and then trying to get it out of the drain is a story.

To Do

Go through your beat sheet and examine each scene for conflict. Write what, exactly, is the conflict of each scene under your description of the scene. If there is no conflict, there is no scene. Sometimes you'll need to group several beats to make a whole scene, so not every beat will have conflict. For example, if you included an establishing shot of a beach, say, as a scene, but really it is just an establishing shot to show you're in Hawaii, group it with the next beat or beats and write what the conflict is for that group of beats.

What You Need

What if you've got a great scene that is really funny, or dramatic, or tear-jerking? If it doesn't move the story along its way, we don't need it. If we don't need it, we don't put it in. No matter how brilliant they are, only necessary scenes are allowed, no side trips to Grandma's house, no stopping to smell the flowers along the way, no trips to the comedy store or theme park — unless they are essential for the story. Bad scenes that move the story forward can be fixed. Great scenes that don't move the story are irreparable. They slow down the movie (or the reader of your script) and tend to make an audience fidget or wonder "what the hell?"

To Do

Read through your beat sheet again (again!) and delete scenes that don't move the story forward or reveal character. If a scene doesn't have conflict, figure out what the conflict should be. If you can't find conflict in that scene, cut it. Be brutal!

I mean it.

How to Rewrite the Scene

As with everything else in writing, for the screen or otherwise, there are as many ways to write a scene as there are writers. That means good as well as bad. That means easy as well as difficult. That means I have some ideas on this subject, but they're not gospel; and to make things more complicated, I'm always changing them. But for now, here's how I suggest you do it when you rewrite.

I've already talked about the scene having a beginning, a middle, and an end. About it having conflict. Now let's talk about the course of that conflict and where we are in it when we enter and leave the scene, and why we're in it in the first place.

Every major player in a scene has an objective — he wants something. As Robin Swicord, screenwriter on *Little Women*, *The Perez Family*, and *Memoirs of a Geisha*, says, "I want. Everything comes from that." Usually, each character wants something different. Hence the conflict. We must also know what the emotion of that character is at the beginning of the scene, what his attitude is, and what his long-term goal is. There's a helluva difference between a scene that starts with everyone pissed off at each other from the get-go and one that starts with laughter. If you know your characters, you'll know what their emotions are at the beginning of the scene — are they happy, sad, angry — and what will happen to them during the scene. Unless they have cause to change (they may or may not), they should maintain that emotion throughout the scene. Actors look at scenes this way (or the good ones do), and they look for hints the writer has given them.

We also need to know what the subject and purpose of the scene is. Yes, it's to move the story forward, first and foremost. But it may also be to shed some light on a character, to reveal information, to provide an obstacle. Know what you want to get across with your scene.

An Actor's POV

According to Don Richardson, the late television director, when an actor looks at a scene, he looks at two key elements to guide him through the scene. One is feeling; the other is purpose. An actor looks at a scene and tries to discern what emotion he has at the beginning of the scene and if that emotion remains the same throughout the scene. It will only change if there is something to change it. He also looks at the character's goal throughout the scene. What is his objective?

It's important to tell the actor what the objective or goal in the scene is and how he feels about it. We do this in a combination of dialogue and description (action). Character is action, action is conflict, conflict is drama. We learn who the character is by how he reacts to the conflict — the obstacles in the way of his achieving his goal.

How do we ensure that this will happen? By making sure there is an opposing force, whether it is the antagonist or simply another person or element which has an opposing goal. In *Platoon*, written by Oliver Stone, the North Vietnamese Army did not want to be captured. They evaded and sabotaged, taunted and hid from the platoon, frustrating them. When the platoon reaches the village looking for the NVA, the main obstacle is language and lack of willingness to cooperate. Conflict in every scene doesn't mean you have to have an argument, just that you have to have opposing goals. When you have opposing goals, characters test their mettle and show who they really are. In this scene, the soldiers get so angry trying to communicate and finding enemy supplies, they end up burning the village to the ground.

The basics are simple. Someone wants something; the other person doesn't want them to have it. In an action scene, that could translate to someone wanting to escape, but the other won't let him without a fight or a chase. Someone wants to kill the enemy; the other is the enemy that wants to kill back. Someone wants to rob a bank; others want to stop him. Someone wants to win a car race; someone else wants to win just as badly. Someone wants to destroy the Death Star; others want to destroy those pesky Rebels. You get the idea. Much of the time the goal is forgotten midway through the action, but the action must be sustained by the conflict — the opposition of the goals.

How does an individual action scene fit into the movie as a whole? And how does the central goal fit into the scene? Remember, every scene must move the story forward. If it doesn't, it's out, no matter how funny, how thrilling, how scary, how daring. The scene serves the story as a whole, except for the first sequence in a James Bond movie which rarely, if ever, has anything to do with the film as a whole. If the underwater fight between the Count of Monte Cristo and his jailer hadn't served the story, it would have been cut.

The scene needs to move the story. Therefore, part of the central goal must be accomplished in the scene. In *The Count of Monte Cristo*, written by Jay Wolpert, based on the novel by Alexandre Dumas, for example, the count must escape to achieve revenge. His goal in the underwater fight scene is to escape. He jumps off the cliff and takes the jailer with him. His goal is still to escape, but his more immediate goal is to get the keys so he can free himself from his chains. Once done, he drowns the jailer as part of his overall revenge. Now he is free to recreate himself and seek revenge on his accuser.

The short-term goal serves the long-term goal. The long-term goal drives the scene's necessity.

Overall, the most important element in the scene is the conflict that drives the action. The conflict is established by the obstacles that prevent the protagonist from reaching his goals.

Now where does your scene start? Okay, it starts at the beginning. No, it has a beginning, it doesn't necessarily start in the beginning. It should, in fact, start as late into the scene as possible and end as soon as it has an ending (not necessarily at the end of the scene). What do I mean by this? Let's take a domestic fight, for example, say between Romeo and Juliet had they lived through that little misunderstanding about the poison. Romeo's got a dead-end job at a supermarket packing bags. Juliet's got a kid at her breast and one on the way. Romeo has been dressed down by the produce manager, and he's angry.

Where do we start the argument over dinner not being ready? (Which is really an argument about him having to be a wage slave and her having no one to talk to all day.) We could start it when he slams the door on entry to their stifling one-bedroom, un-air-conditioned hellhole in North Hollywood. We could start it when he sees her lying on the couch flipping channels with the remote. Or we could wait until he sits down at the table (not set for dinner) and starts pounding his fists. All, actually, are good starting points depending on the ending point you have in mind. I vote for the fists banging on the table, but there's no set place to begin this scene. It all depends on what you want to say.

Where do we end this revelation of domestic bliss that confronts teenagers who get married on impulse? If we had started it when the door slammed, we could have ended it at the fists hitting the table. If we start it at the fists hitting the table, we can end it when he throws the dish of spaghetti (again!) to the floor, or when he clips her one, or when he stomps out the door. You decide. It depends on what you want to say about Romeo and Juliet, where you are in the movie, what their emotions are, where you started the scene in the first place. I'd end it before he left the house — we've seen that, and we know he's going to do that. But that's me. I like shorthand in my movies.

To Do

One more time through the beat sheet, this time to note what the protagonist of the scene (which could be anyone, not necessarily the protagonist of your movie) wants. What is his emotion at the start of the scene? And what is the purpose of the scene?

Just in case I haven't mentioned it sufficiently, let me underline it again: *The element most new (and many experienced) screenwriters leave out of their scenes is conflict.* Without conflict, there is no drama. Without drama (even in a comedy), there is no story. Without conflict, there is no movement. No change. Conflict is the key element of the scene.

The Sequence

Sometimes it's easier to think of a movie in terms of the main sequences. A sequence is a group of scenes that all have a common flow and purpose. They might take place over a period of time and in several locations, but they have a thematic unity. And, of course, they have filmic structure, which is to say, they have a seven-point structure as well.

Often, sequences are found at important story points. The ordinary life of a movie can be something boring that you just have to sit through, or it can provide interesting and informative moments that make you want to see the rest of the film. If that sequence is done right, it can help launch a franchise.

Let's look at *Die Hard*, screenplay by Jeb Stuart and Steven E. de Souza, based on the novel by Roderick Thorp. The box office that *Die Hard* generated convinced Fox to sink money into a sequel, and they were well enough rewarded by that one to want to come up with a third, fourth, and fifth. Why? Action movies are a dime a dozen. Okay, $50 to $100 million apiece. But most of the big ones make money based on the box-office pull of their stars and/or amazing action.

Fox didn't have a big star in Willis at the time. He'd done TV and was popular enough, but he hadn't established himself as an action star, just as a wisecracking romantic TV character — a long way from Schwarzenneger or Stallone, the reigning action stars of the time. What made this film big? We cared. And we cared enough to tell our friends to see it, and millions of them did. And when did we learn to care in a nonstop action film?

In the first ten minutes.

The opening shot of *Die Hard*, over titles, is that of a jetliner landing at LAX. Nothing new there, just establishing. But almost immediately we meet John McClane, though we will not know his name for some time. We also don't see his face immediately, just his hand gripping the armrest for dear life as the plane lands. This tells us something important about John — he either has a fear of flying or of heights or both. And he is a human being, a hero with a flaw. Characters without flaws are not as likable as characters with them, and though it isn't uncommon for an action hero to be practically flawless, the ones with imperfections are the ones we really root for.

The opening scenes (sequence) serve to tell us about the central character and his current condition. His ordinary life.

Then we switch scenes to set up his wife, the emotional relationship that John will have at stake in this story. We're not exactly sure what the situation is — separation or divorce — but we know it isn't good between them when she slams the picture of their family face down on the desk. We see, though, that she is a woman of some means and power: She has a nanny at home and a prestigious office at work. This is her ordinary life scene.

Then it's back to John, whose name we learn from the sign a driver waiting at the gate is holding. So exposition is coming in bits and pieces. The driver asks some pointed questions, and John admits he's married, that his wife moved to L.A. six months ago for a job, and so on. The driver asks all the questions the audience wants to ask. We're beginning to know Mr. J. McClane. We know the state of his marriage, his career, her career (though it's vague as to what exactly she does), why he didn't follow her to L.A., and his attitudes.

We also know he loves his kids (the big teddy bear). All this before the main titles are over.

Now the writers use Argyle (De'voreaux White), the limo driver, to help us understand what McClane's goal is. He lays out a scenario for the reunion: "The lady sees you, you run into each other's arms, and you live happily ever after." McClane responds laconically, "I can live with that." That's what he wants. That's his goal, his motivation for all that will come later. That, in addition to the freeing of the hostages, is what he must accomplish in this film.

We're still in the first ten minutes when McClane enters the Nakatomi Building and finds it quiet. He finds out at the front desk that his wife no longer uses her married name at work, so we learn something about her as well, something that will come back several times and pay off well in the end. It irks him that she uses her maiden name.

Soon he's met by his wife, Holly (Bonnie Bedelia), and escorted into her office where her colleague is sniffing cocaine. Holly is emotional about the reunion, but controlled in front of her colleague.

So far, it could be any relationship movie. But when we see a large truck fill the screen and hear foreboding music, we know that the truck is going to be trouble for McClane and that his world is about to change.

Back to the relationship, Holly invites John to stay in the spare room, but the conversation soon turns into an argument, picking up where they, presumably, left off months ago. This is the inciting incident of the sequence. Soon after Holly is called away (again, business interrupts their relationship), the intruders take charge of the building, shutting down its systems and closing off its exits.

Meanwhile, John is barefoot in the bathroom grasping at the carpet with his toes as his seat neighbor on the plane had suggested. Then shots ring out, and we're on our way, fully invested in the hero and his dual mission (because now we know he's going to have to save his wife as well as his relationship with her). This is the end of act 1 of the sequence. He has a goal — to find her.

Now the violence — whoops! I mean action — has a larger purpose. While saving a group of hostages is a good and worthy purpose, if we don't know them or the savior's stake, we don't really care enough to sit through a two-hour movie. But if there's a relationship hanging by a thread, then we give a damn. Setting up the characters and the situation, and getting us to care about what happens, is the job of the first ten minutes. If it isn't done then, we don't usually read (or watch) past that.

As you can see, even in an action picture as intense as *Die Hard*, we watch primarily because we care about the characters. And we create the audience's perception of our central characters in the opening sequences.

In *Thelma & Louise* there is a fine sequence that makes up the inciting incident and another that forms the midpoint of the movie. If you haven't seen this movie in a few years, rent it, download it, or stream it and watch carefully. It's a superbly constructed film. Its midpoint sequence, for example, focuses on Thelma's midpoint change, though it crosscuts with Louise and her boyfriend.

The ordinary life of that sequence is the scene in which Louise gives Thelma the money that Jimmy, Louise's boyfriend, has brought her.

The inciting incident of the sequence is when J.D. comes to Thelma's door, all wet and seductive. Thelma takes him in and her life changes. Darryl and she had been together since she was fourteen. He was the only man she had ever known. Now she learns a thing or two about sex with J.D.

The end of act 1 of the sequence is when J.D. takes Thelma's wedding ring and dumps it in a glass. At this stage, he's the protagonist. He's driving the action. He has a plan.

The midpoint of the sequence is when Thelma shows up the next morning in the coffee shop lightheaded and drunk with sex. That is, until Louise asks her where the money is.

The low point is the discovery that J.D. has stolen it. Now the story spins off in a new direction because this is the low point of the midpoint (confused yet?). Thelma wants to maintain that "it's okay," but Louise says, "It's not okay. None of this is okay."

Geena Davis, Thelma & Louise, *written by Callie Khouri, directed by*
Ridley Scott (Pathé Entertainment, 1991).

The final challenge of the sequence is when Thelma takes charge and
gets Louise packed and into the car.

The return to normal life for the sequence is when they take off in the
car, resuming their life on the road.

To Do

Now, review your beat sheet once again (see how handy they are?) and
group your scenes into sequences that make sense. Some rearranging might
be in order, and not all scenes will fit into a sequence. That's all right. Now
it's time to rewrite the scenes, keeping in mind all that you've learned up to
this point: The scene must have a purpose. It must have a protagonist and
an antagonist. It must have conflict. It has a seven-point structure, though
it could start late and end early. It may be part of a sequence with its own
seven points.

At this stage, you can do the exercise or you can wait until we've discussed description and dialogue. I'd do the exercise.

DIALOGUE:
TEXT, SUBTEXT, AND NO TEXT

Dialogue is one way to delineate your characters. This is especially true for your protagonist. He or she should have his or her own way of talking. And it's not just what they say, but how they say it. You've also probably noticed that your character's voice changed as you got to know her. It's a good bet to say that she sounds different at the beginning of your story than at the end. So go through the script reading only the protagonist's dialogue. As you go, look for ways to unify the voice of the character, to make it stand out, to make it tell us who your character really is. Does the dialogue tell us who this person is just by the way she talks? In other words, is there a vocabulary she favors? Is her level of education obvious? Do we hear regionalisms (if appropriate) or an accent? Do we hear her age and social register? (Social register refers to the subtle changes we make in our speech according to whom we're talking. More on this a little later in this chapter.)

Some screenwriting programs have a feature that will let you print only the "sides" (relevant pages) for any particular character. That will help you focus on your character in context.

For a good example of consistent and stand-out dialogue, read Shakespeare's dialogue in *Shakespeare in Love*, then read the rest of the script. Here screenwriters Marc Norman and Tom Stoppard clearly delineate all characters with dialogue but do an especially good job with Shakespeare, who often speaks as he writes in his plays. There's a unique freshness in his language. No one else sounds like him. Can you say that about your protagonist?

To Do

Read through the central character's dialogue without stopping to read other characters so you can hear just the one voice in your head. Make changes as necessary.

It's not only a matter of how your character speaks, but what he says. Dialogue is at its most interesting when the character's true intent lies under the words he says, in the subtext. A character is flat when he speaks the subtext, saying what he really means or feels.

Subtext in dialogue is when one thing is said but the real meaning is something else. Who among us hasn't talked about things in front of (our) children that we didn't want them to understand? We talk about, say, how Betty, a very sensuous person, likes to have sex with a range of international partners. We might say that she likes to sample … uh, coffee from many different lands. She likes American "coffee," French "coffee," Turkish "coffee," but really prefers Italian "coffee." We understand what is meant, but our children do not (we hope).

Sometimes a character does this intentionally in the film, sometimes not. When the lynch mob gathers at the jail in *To Kill a Mockingbird* (screenplay by Horton Foote, based on the novel by Harper Lee), Atticus' (Gregory Peck) young daughter Scout (Mary Badham) defuses the situation by talking to Mr. Cunningham about several things — the hickory nuts he'd brought over, his son, and other subjects. On the surface, she's just trying to be friendly. Deeper than that, she's showing the mob, and Cunningham in particular, that they're all part of a community that relies on each other, that helps each other out, and that her father in particular is a pillar of this community in the truest sense. Cunningham realizes he can't move against Finch now, and he tells the others to come away with him.

Scout didn't try to tell them the underlying truths; she just talked like they were assumed. Foote knew what he was doing. The innocence of the text and the child contrast with the menace of the mob.

In a film, this kind of dialogue can keep your audience on its toes and add character to your characters and spark to your scenes. Look at *The Godfather: Part II*, screenplay by Francis Ford Coppola based on the novel by Mario Puzo, when Tom Hagen, the Robert Duvall character, talks about Roman times with the turncoat Pentangeli, or *The Big Sleep*, screenplay by William Faulkner based on the novel by Raymond Chandler, when Bogart's character talks to Bacall's character about horse racing. It's not about horse racing at all but, again, about sex. Nor was Duvall having a historical chat about the Romans. He was negotiating Pentangeli's exit strategy, a clean way for him to commit suicide and have the mob take care of his family.

To Do

Find places in your screenplay where you can change on-the-nose dialogue into subtextual dialogue.

The Defining Line

There's one more line of dialogue that is key to your character. It's often called the character line. It's something your protagonist says that really nails who he is and what his journey has been or will be. UCLA's Jim Schmerer tells his students to look for some place in their screenplay where they can have the major character actually reveal himself to the audience. In addition to telling the reader and audience who this person is, it's something that an actor will glom onto, be interested in, when he reads the screenplay. When an actor gets interested, the studios get interested.

For example, in *The Verdict*, screenplay by David Mamet, Paul Newman's character, Frank Galvin, gives us his character in one speech when he says, "I came in here to take your money. (beat) I brought snapshots to show you. So I could get your money. (to Young Priest, waving away document) I can't take it. If I take it. If I take that money I'm lost. I'm just going to be a rich ambulance chaser. (beat; pleading for understanding) I can't do it. I can't take it." That speech sets up his character and the fight he's about to enter into.

Michael's line in *Tootsie*, when he says, "I'm a better man as a woman than I was as a man," tells the audience just how far Michael has come. In *Dirty Harry*, screenplay by Harry Julian Fink, Rita M. Fink, and Dean Riesner, the infamous line that Harry says to a perp to whose head he's holding his pistol has entered the language, but it also tells us a lot about the character. "Make my day," says he's looking for an excuse to shoot the man, that he has his own set of rules to play by, and that he'll do what he needs to do to get what he wants.

Finding the line for your central character will help you to know him better. If you know the underlying reasons why a character acts the way he does — not the plot points or what he does, but why he does it, what's inside that character, what's driving him or her — it impacts each scene in everything he says and does. If you know this, you will have your audience emotionally involved in the character.

Here's another example. In *The Maltese Falcon*, screenplay by John Huston based on the novel by Dashiell Hammett, it looks like Sam Spade will do anything inside or outside the law to reach his goal — money, the falcon. In the final scene, he turns to the woman he loves and tells her he's going to turn her in for killing his partner. "Don't believe I'm as crooked as they say. It's good for business." At that moment, we know he was a moral detective, and everything was geared towards finding out who killed his partner.

Even an antagonist can have a similar line. Doesn't this line sum up Arnold Schwarzenegger's character in *The Terminator*, written by James Cameron and Gale Anne Hurd, completely: "I'll be back"?

As you read through the dialogue for the protagonist, look for a line like this, and if there isn't one, write one. It will help you focus on who your character is and what he will do.

To Do

Write that one line of dialogue that says it all for your character.

Other Subtle Dialogue Issues

We all know that we speak differently to a police officer than to our significant other. You speak differently to a doctor than to the nurse, to a priest than to your child, to your boss than to a co-worker. We sometimes call this social register.

Another way to describe this is in terms of status, which is much more fluid within a conversation and can change in an instant. Low status is characterized by subordination or deference to others. High status is characterized by superiority, primacy, or domination over others.

Examples

- Very low status: If you're not using it, could you please pass me your pen.

- Low status: Please pass me your pen.

- High status: Give me the pen.

- Very high status: The pen. Now.

- Very low status: How are you? Are you thirsty? Do you want me to get you something to drink?

- Low status: If you're thirsty, let me get you something to drink.

- High Status: It looks like you're thirsty. I'm going to get you something to drink.

- Very high status: You're thirsty. Go get something to drink.

In a conversation, status is always changing. Normally, it's instinctive.

To Do

Write in one or two lines of dialogue about the following situation according to the status of the character in relationship to the one listening: asking someone to repay a debt.

• If the speaker has very low status in that situation.

• If the speaker has low status in that situation.

• If the speaker has high status in that situation.

• If the speaker has very high status in that situation.

Locale

Locale can also affect dialogue. The atmosphere of a place can lend and demand status. Think about architecture. What buildings and surroundings are designed to make you feel small, as if you're in the presence of something bigger than you? Saint Peter's Basilica, the Capitol building in Washington, the office of the CEO of a large company: Don't they all affect how you feel? If you feel differently, you speak differently.

Surroundings and situations also manipulate status. Any human community does it — the United Nations, the music industry, a group of friends in a bar. One of the things that make a community is the intent to define status and the role of status. This decision is collective and based on the values and necessities of the group. A man talking about the smell of a rose can be appreciated by a garden club, but will be laughed at in the local bar. A person who blows himself up is a terrorist to one group and a martyr to another. How he talks about it in the online video afterwards is one thing. How he explains it to his mother would be another.

Status is very fluid. Imagine a chief of state talking to an audience. She has the highest status, right? But what happens if a delegate has a heart attack? Now a doctor comes forward. She has the highest status because everyone is waiting for her to take charge of the situation. So the status has changed because the circumstances of the room have changed.

This happens in conversations. One person knows nothing about sports, so when the conversation is about sports, she has low status. But let's say she's an engineer. Then, talking about how to build a space station, she will have much higher status in a group of normal people.

From place to place, community to community, moment to moment, we are always fighting for status on a playing field that is constantly changing. Again, watch the scene in *Shakespeare in Love* in which Wessex tells Viola that her father has bought him for her and they are to be married. His status changes from moment to moment, as does his tone, as the power shifts from her to him.

To Do

Check all your scenes to ensure that people are speaking with the appropriate status.

For more on dialogue, be sure to read *Talk the Talk: A Dialogue Workshop for Scriptwriters* by Penny Penniston.

MAKING DESCRIPTIONS
LEAP OFF THE PAGE

Here's one of the basic contradictions a writer has to face. You know that a reader, probably not the producer, is going to be the first person at the production company or studio to read your script, so you have to impress this person. (A reader is someone an executive, agent, or producer hires to read a script and write a report that includes an analysis, a summary, and a recommendation. A reader is the first person empowered to say no to your work. And she usually does because that's the safest thing to do.) We know that motion pictures are all about what you see on screen, so you'd think that the descriptive passages of a script would be important. And they are. But readers often skip through them to get to the dialogue because they think, sometimes correctly, that the character is shaped by the dialogue. And dialogue is easier to read. But harder to write.

Does that mean you shouldn't pay attention to description? No. Does it mean that you shouldn't write visually? No, on the contrary. You should still make the reader see the movie as best you can, and that's where your writing style for descriptive paragraphs will pay off.

Before you start to rewrite all the descriptions in your script, let's talk a little about what your pages should look like and why. First of all, pity the poor script readers. They generally read two, sometimes three, scripts per day. Their eyes get tired. They need white space to rest them on. If your script reduces their eye fatigue, they will automatically be happier with your script. So you want to make their job easier by giving them lots of white space.

No, you will not sell a script based on the amount of white space on a page. But you may lose the reader's interest if he or she has to plough through dense and long paragraphs. You want to make your paragraphs as short and succinct as possible. Michael Goldenberg, who wrote the screenplays for *Contact, Peter Pan, Harry Potter and the Order of the Phoenix*, and *Green Lantern*, says you want to make your description "efficient but provocative." Jack Epps Jr., who co-wrote *Top Gun, Legal Eagles*, and *Dick Tracy*, urges writers to "write in small fragments using verbs instead of nouns."

No one has ever been accused of having too little description. Screenplays are terse, filled with short phrases emphasizing verbs always — *always* — in the present tense.

```
Connor drags himself to the bed. Falls. Checks his
arm. Blood spurts out of his wrist. He slams his other
palm on it. Nearly faints.
```

Short declarative sentences. Fragments. Lots of verbs. But the scene is clear as a bell, isn't it? You can see it, can't you? You don't need to know what kind of bed it is, or even what Connor looks like. You see the action, and that's what counts. Let the make-up artist, the set designer, the production designer, the wardrobe designer, the director of photography, and the director fill in the rest. Let them do their jobs. Your job is to make them see the film, see the action, and move on.

But what would Mrs. Thrall, my twelfth-grade English teacher, say about using fragments (not to mention starting a sentence with a conjunction)? I don't care what she would say. (Though, believe me, I respect her and all she taught me.) This is screenwriting, not a critical analysis of *Moby Dick*. You don't have to follow the conventions of English usage, but you do have to use English in a way that gets people excited about your story. So you use whatever works.

On the other hand, you can't sound like you don't know how to use the conventions of modern English. You have to know the rules to break the rules. You must be correct in subject-verb agreement, use of your/you're, their/there/they're, and such confusing things as the difference between lay and lie (if you don't know, look it up; it'll stay with you longer). That means spelling and punctuation, too, though you can certainly bend the rules with punctuation. You don't want readers to misjudge your screenplay because it has grammatical mistakes where it shouldn't. Making mistakes on purpose is one thing. Making them because of laziness or ignorance is another.

How will the reader know the difference? She will, believe me. Just like you can spot sloppy production values like a mike hanging in a scene, unless that's done on purpose in a mockumentary.

Using Visual Subtext to Underscore Your Meaning

As we discussed, subtext is the meaning underlying the words or actions. Words and actions can have apparent meaning and, in so doing, serve the story. But they can also have meaning below the text, meaning not directly spelled out, that can also serve the story. Why do we care about subtext? Because anything that can make a movie richer, that can give it more depth, texture, complexity, is a good thing. It will reach people on more than one level and give them a deeper appreciation of what you're trying to get across. Especially if you do it in action.

Let's look at *To Kill a Mockingbird* for subtext. The scene with the rabid dog is a good example of subtext in physical action. We know that Atticus (the Gregory Peck character) is a peacemaker, yet we are surprised to learn that he's such a good shot that the sheriff gives him a rifle to shoot the rabid dog. It's a surprise even to his children that he's the "best shot in town." What are we to make of this, and why do we need it since it's not about the main course of action?

It tells us that Atticus *chooses* to be a peacemaker. He has the ability to defend himself and his children if he wants to, but he chooses words instead of bullets to do so. This will come into play later when he's confronted on the jailhouse steps by the mob. He could have brought a rifle, assuming he owned one, but he brought only his words. Just as he warned Scout not to fight no matter what anyone says, he never stoops to violence or anger when attacked verbally, or even when he's spit on. More character.

Of course, there is always the knowledge, running below the text, that he could choose differently. It may even be inferred (here's another pair of words to look up — infer and imply) that he spent time in the army. That creates a tension of its own — will he use his skills when the children are in danger?

How Long Is an Action Paragraph?

Short.

As short as one word. Maybe two. Just like a sentence. Whatever it takes to give your words kick. An impact. Play fast and loose with what Mrs. Thrall taught you (I can see her spinning in her grave now). You don't need a subject sentence with several sentences supporting it. All you need is the action. A rule of thumb (a short thumb) is to keep paragraphs under four lines. If you have a longer need, break the paragraphs up into shots — visualize the scene. How would the director cut it? Describe each shot briefly and move on.

That's visual storytelling.

That's what works in a screenplay.

Read the following excerpt from a children's movie and see if you can visualize the individual shots.

```
FADE IN:

EXT. SOCCER FIELD - DAY

A ball flies past a thirteen year old GOALIE and
into the net.

                    CARLOS (O.S.)
          Goooooaaaaaal!
```

Then...

CARLOS RANDALL

11, shaggy, straight black hair, baggy soccer uni-
form. He is not on the field but standing with a
group of other TEAM MEMBERS, all bigger than he is,
YELLING ad lib encouragement to their TEAMMATE who
has just scored.

Groups of SPECTATORS watch and cheer. Among them,

AMANDA,

Carlos' mother, 30s, dark, sunken eyes that have
seen some pain. Carlos' TEAMMATES and OPPONENTS re-
position themselves on the field.

The furor dies down, and Carlos and a few other
boys sit down on the bench again.

The COACH, balding, squat, but tightly muscled,
makes a T with his hands and...

          COACH
    Time out!

A WHISTLE blows and the game stops.

          COACH
    Chen and Williams, go in
    for Charles and Stein. Go
    go go...

The TWO KIDS race onto the field. They run to
their teammates...

```
                CARLOS
        Coach! What about me?
        I'm ready.

                COACH
        I know you are, Carlos.
        Hang on. Soon.

Carlos turns away, disappointed, as the TWO KIDS who
were playing trot off the field to the bench and take
their seats next to him.
```

Some Other Rules

Screenplays are always written in the present tense to give you a sense of immediacy. It's happening right now, right here. On the screen.

That also means you only write what you see on screen. You can't write the characters' histories (background) because the viewer (as opposed to the reader) won't see that on screen. You can't write inner thoughts. You can't write emotions that aren't played out. You can't write plans or hidden desires. You can only write what the viewer will see. That means you have to find a way to express all of that in action and dialogue.

To Do

Go through the descriptive paragraphs in your screenplay and see if you can take out all the adverbs and as many adjectives and nouns as possible. Shorten your sentences. Shorten your paragraphs. Take out what can't be seen or heard in the theater.

The Way They Used to Do It

In the heyday of the silent film, the only way to get your point across in a scene was to *show* it. Sure, there were title cards, but the story was developed with actions and images. The actors developed a style to express emotion, and words weren't needed. With the advent of sound, film acting became more subtle. A minute change in a facial expression could cause or be caused by a word or line of dialogue.

Still, today, even with completely naturalistic sound and lighting, the most effective way to tell your story is with actions and images. They're universal. They're not lost in translation in the foreign market.

Sure, it seems more efficient just to tell the audience what you want them to know by putting the information in dialogue. But nothing is more boring than sitting through five minutes of verbal exposition. Especially if you can *show* it in one simple image. What's more effective, showing the Death Star rotating in space or Luke Skywalker saying, "Look, there's a huge man-made planet that looks impenetrable"?

Okay, that's the easy stuff. How do you show a character's background or thoughts? Sometimes you *will* have to resort to dialogue, but it's better if you don't. What if you want to tell us that he grew up on a ranch? Try describing worn cowboy boots, a way of walking, and maybe even a little bit of "chaw" in his cheek. What if you want to show he's angry? He spits a bit of the chaw in an inappropriate place. What if you want us to know he's planning to compete in the rodeo today? He practices with a lariat.

All pretty easy, I admit. I chose my examples carefully, but look to the *behavior* of your character to tell the story. Write description an actor can play. Yes, you can say he's angry because he can play angry, but it's even more effective to the reader if he charges into the bunkhouse, tips over a bunk bed, and kicks it to splinters.

Just about any emotion can be played by an actor, especially if you give him some actions to work with. Thoughts and plans are much harder, so you will have to find a way to externalize them or put them into dialogue. Building models, unfolding plans, surveying a plot of land (not literally, just looking it over), or even just picking up a travel brochure can say a lot about your story. Maybe not everything, but a lot. Have your people *do*, not talk.

To Do

Find a scene that is heavy in dialogue and try to express it completely in action and description. I said try. It may not be possible, but in the eighty or so classes I've used this exercise, it's produced hundreds of superior scenes relying on images and actions alone.

When you've finished that scene, go through your whole movie and apply what you've learned in this chapter to your descriptive paragraphs. Make them short. Punchy. Verb heavy. Use them as substitutes for dialogue whenever possible so that your pages aren't "too talky."

LIFE SUPPORT
FOR YOUR PROTAGONIST

Let's talk about supporting players. If your story has only a protagonist and an antagonist, it's going to be pretty thin. They need friends, colleagues, allies in their battle. And the old adage, "You're known by the company you keep," is very true in film. It's one way we learn who the central character is — by the people he surrounds himself with. Are your supporting characters doing all they can do to support your protagonist and the story?

Let's look at *The Wizard of Oz*, that veritable textbook of screenwriting. The supporting characters not only help Dorothy in her quest to return home, but also represent parts of Dorothy's personality, as Chris Vogler has pointed out in his essential book, *The Writer's Journey*. That is, they represent parts of her personality that need development. The cowardly lion helps Dorothy to face things the way they are and not run away from them — a lesson he must learn, too. The tin man underscores Dorothy's need for empathy with others. The straw man represents her need to use her own wits instead of always relying on her aunt and uncle to get her out of scrapes. Even the good witch stands for something inside Dorothy — her innate goodness and love of her home and family. She just needs a little reminding that there's no place like home.

And the Wicked Witch — doesn't she represent the selfishness that Dorothy needs to purge herself of if she is to return home as a responsible adult? Isn't this her flaw, the one she must overcome in a final act of selflessness in front of the Wizard?

Jack Haley, Ray Bolger, Judy Garland, and Bert Lahr, The Wizard of Oz, *screenplay by Noel Langley, Florence Ryerson, and Edgar Allan Woolf, based on a novel by L. Frank Baum, directed by Victor Fleming (MGM, 1939).*

Each of these characters has his or her own arc. Each shows us who she is by what she does and says. Each seeks to be validated for the trait she most admires (except for the Wicked Witch, of course), and each (except Glinda, the good witch) displays that trait and receives an award from the Wizard to prove she has it. By the time Dorothy reaches the Wizard, she has proven she has all three traits she needs and has overcome her selfishness.

In *The Green Mile*, screenplay by Frank Darabont based on the novella by Stephen King, many of the supporting players are there to contrast with Paul as a way of bringing out his character, which, though upright and respectable, is somewhat drab. In one sequence in the film, we see various kinds of behavior and dialogue that set up Paul (the character played by Tom Hanks) and show him to be a compassionate man despite the fact that he supervises the warehousing, and then execution, of prisoners. The people around him are interesting in themselves and create interest in the movie for the viewer.

Around scene 33 of the shooting script, Toot, a trusty played by Harry Dean Stanton, begins the rehearsal of an upcoming execution of a Native American. We learn just who he is in a pair of lines: "Sittin' down, sittin' down, rehearsing now! Everybody settle!" He's comfortable enough with his keeper to feel free to mimic him irreverently. His repetitive speech tells us that he may be missing a few marbles. He makes us laugh in the midst of what should be supremely solemn. And, eventually, he gives Paul the opportunity to point that out, as he does at the end of scene 51 (when he talks about trying not to laugh in church). Paul, by contrast, is a compassionate, serious person with respect for human dignity.

In this sequence Darabont also further sets up Percy's (Doug Hutchison) evil when we see he learns about the wetting of the sponge. Later, his brutal act (not to be confused with the respectable Brutal, the David Morse character) further underlines Paul's innate goodness. We've suspected Percy for some time and have been wondering since the previous scene how his evil is going to manifest itself. Soon we'll know. If Percy is evil, Paul is good.

During the final part of the rehearsal, Paul's compassion and tolerance of Toot is underscored with a roll of his eyes and a choice to ignore the intruding mouse. Contrast this with Percy's behavior in the previous sequence when the mouse outruns him and his traps.

Paul is one determined and compassionate man. How do we know? By how he reacts to the supporting characters and by how they stand in stark contrast to him.

What do your supporting characters support? Are they sounding boards for your central character? Are they contrasts? Are they really facets of the central character, as in *The Wizard of Oz*, there to help her grow and become the woman she needs to be?

To Do

Make sure each supporting character has a purpose and that you know what that purpose is. List each supporting character of importance (you don't need to write down characters such as POLICE OFFICER 2) and what his purpose in the script is. If you don't know why he's there, cut or replace him with somebody who has purpose.

Developing Their Personalities

Now you have all the supporting characters that you need, but they just seem to stand there like pillars, holding up their end of the bargain. Nothing special. Okay, maybe one or two are special. But how do you make them stand out? How do you separate your supporting characters from the people that just come and go in your protagonist's life?

The easy way? Give them a quirk: something unusual about their dress code, their speech (either how they speak or what they talk about), even the way they use their hands. This allows you to paint a picture of a character in very few words, while still giving their appearance the impact that you want. Part of that impact is how the supporting character sets off your protagonist. Look at *Beverly Hills Cop*, story by Danilo Bach and Daniel Petrie Jr., screenplay by Daniel Petrie Jr. I still remember the boutique barista, Serge, played by Bronson Pinchot, for his accent, dialogue, and mannerisms. He's one small character who served as a foil for Eddie Murphy in that scene, but he stands out from the crowd. He helped increase the comedy in that film, always a good thing (if intentional).

How about a supporting player with a much more important role? Think of the breakthrough role for Brad Pitt in *Thelma & Louise*. As J.D., he stood out because of his cowboy hat, his clothes, and his sixpack, not to mention that slow, seductive drawl. We didn't have to be with him for a minute before we knew what went on inside his head and what his motives were. He had several appearances in the film, and they all had a function. He was essential for Thelma's sexual revolution. The skills he taught her regarding holdups was job training that led to an escalation of the action after the midpoint. He served a definite set of functions and helped the central character develop so the story could charge on. Did he change? Probably not. But he didn't have to.

Not all supporting characters have to have their own arc. In the best of movies, many of them do, but not all. In action movies, few do, and it doesn't matter. Often, even the protagonist doesn't change. (Isn't Bond still Bond after all these years? Okay, the new Bond is vulnerable, but he soon reverts to form.)

One essential supporting character was Han Solo in *Star Wars*. He's a hard-boiled space jockey who's in it for the money. But, as Leia tells him, if he's in it only for the money, that's all he'll get. We see him slowly change from a mercenary to a mentor to a hero in the course of the film.

What should you be doing to make sure that your supporting characters are not only doing their job, but making an impression? Yes, a movie is about the protagonist's struggle, but it's also about his world and the people in it. So let's make those people stand out in the service of the story.

To Do

Go through your story and identify the supporting characters who are most important. Beef up their screen presence by giving them a quirk of some sort. Make them stand out. Have the quirk relate to their personality or function regarding your protagonist or your antagonist.

PARING IT DOWN

I can absolutely guarantee you, based on almost thirty years of experience, that the second thing a reader (be she a reader, development executive, agent, producer, or studio head) will do when she gets your script, is thumb through to the end to see what the page count is. The first, of course, is to read the title and name, possibly your agent's name and contact info. But the most important issue for her will be the length.

What? Length over quality? You mean to tell me you'll be judged on length? Not exactly. Here's how it works. Readers read two or three scripts a day. A long one makes the day long. It will be read later in the day or put off until tomorrow. When tomorrow comes, it will be read later in the day or put off until the next day. Wouldn't you do that?

Development execs, producers, and studio executives know that audiences will sit for ninety minutes to two hours to watch a film. Distributors and exhibitors like films that length because you can fit more showings in a day than with a three-hour film. More showings, more money. So which script would they like to read first, the 100-page script or the 150-page script? Yes, I know, *The Green Mile* was 185 pages. But you're not Frank Darabont, and neither am I. They're gonna look at the page count.

And that page count will influence their attitude when they begin reading. They can't help it. So you want to make them eager to read your work, not dread it. Ideally, then, you want your script to come in under 120 pages, preferably closer to 110. For some genres, it should even be shorter — I wrote scripts for children's films that needed to be in the low 80s. A good comedy might be 95. An epic might be a little longer, but unless you're Oliver Stone, I'd keep it short. If you find yourself edging over 120, it's time to take a serious look at how to lose a little weight. As a matter of fact, I've never read a first draft that wouldn't be improved by taking 10% off it. Even though you've polished and shaped, and the diamond is clear and all facets are shining, you could still take a little off the top and sides (to mix metaphors).

The First Step to Page Reduction

Cut out all carbohydrates. No, sorry, that's the diet you'll have to go on after you finish this draft because you will have gained so much weight from being cooped up in front of your computer for months on end. The first thing you'll need to do is go back to your beat sheet and look over the beats. Does every single one of them move the story forward or reveal something crucial about your protagonist? Preferably, each beat does both. If not, try to combine some scenes. If a scene does neither, cut it. Be ruthless. If you're not sure, take the scene out for a moment, read the scene before and the scene after without the scene in question. Do you lose anything? Does the story still make sense? Then leave it out. If you can get by with just a little additional work in the preceding or following scene, then do that. If there's no way in hell your movie can move forward without that scene, then leave it in.

Michael Goldenberg says, "Cutting is the most powerful tool you have." Use it.

To Do

Cut 10% of the scenes in your movie by combining them, adjusting them, or deleting them altogether.

Here's the original beat sheet a colleague of mine did for a direct-to-DVD children's movie. As a beat sheet, it's a little more fleshed out than most, so it was hard to tell what was needed and what wasn't. I suggested some cuts to streamline the action, keeping in mind that a movie of this type is just a little over eighty minutes long. First, his draft. Then his revised draft, with about 10% cut out. Some of what he cut he later put into other scenes in dialogue or action.

The Bike Squad
Beat Sheet by Martín Olmedo

Sean, 10, watches one of the *Star Wars* movies on his computer. His mother calls him from downstairs for breakfast. Sean yells angrily, "I'm busy." He gets an instant message from "Kbeat": A friend has lodged a Frisbee on a neighbor's roof and is going to get in trouble if they don't retrieve it.

Sean tears through the kitchen, grabbing food, whirling as he downs a quick OJ. Mom tries to make him slow down, have a real breakfast. But he can't waste any time — there's a Bike Squad emergency.

Sean leaves house at a run, putting helmet on. Ignores neighbor boy, Tom, who tries to flag him down. Bikes down the street.

Raffi, in a hurry, feeds himself and his younger brother, Ben, breakfast, fields his nosy questions, then flies out the door, grabbing his helmet. Bikes down the street.

Kathy, in the midst of playing a major drum solo, hears Mom screaming. Stops playing. Mom tells her she promised not to practice more than one hour per day. Time's up. Kathy's reluctant to stop, then realizes she's late. Bikes down the street.

Three cyclists converge — fall in behind Sean. They stop to talk about which route to take. Race to the house where they attempt rescue of a Frisbee. They try to climb a trellis. The owner of the house comes out and threatens them — they're going to fall and he'll have to pay. No way is he going to let that happen.

They ride through the park on the way to their clubhouse. People enjoying the park, especially seniors and children. Some kids a year or two older play touch football. Kathy notices Tom, asks Sean about him. It's a sore subject — Tom dropped him for his in-group friends. They're in different worlds now.

Tom is in the huddle with his team. He tries to call a play, but one of the other kids asks him why Sean snubbed him. Tom says it's a long story. He doesn't want to talk about it.

In their park secret meeting place, there's a debriefing about the Frisbee incident. Ben intrudes. Raffi sends him home.

Construction noise stops their meeting. Workers put up a notice of a conditional use permit meeting. The workers tell them Rosebud Electronics Company wants to build a factory on the site. Can't be, Sean says. It's public land. Worker says company wants to swap larger plot of land on edge of town. Kathy stops her fidgeting long enough to do a square foot calculation, a tax calculation, a tax credit calculation — the deal makes sense.

The kids all sit around a picnic table at the park where they bring out their snacks and water bottles. Kathy informs them of the calorie content of each of their snacks and they argue as to which is best for them. They're all on edge because of what could happen to their park.

Sean argues with his father about the company's plans. But Dad knew about, and is in favor of, the swap. Says the whole Chamber of Commerce is in favor: It's going to be great for urban renewal, increased property values, and taxes to pay for schools. It'll provide for jobs in a depressed economy. Good for everyone, especially him — he'll supply plumbing fixtures. Sean's POV — kids need a place to have fun. Family place. Why can't they have a factory out of town?

Sean plays a video game in his room with Ben looking over his shoulder. Ben is making his own set of sound effects. Sean tries to get him to leave him alone. He's got to think. Ben asks him if playing a game means he's thinking.

Frederic Stone, the president and CEO of Rosebud Electronics, makes a presentation to the Chamber of Commerce. When objections are brought up, he says if it's too much hassle, he'll just cancel the deal, unload the property, and take his jobs and influx of capital to another, less difficult, town. Sean's father leads the audience in applauding him and assures him they're behind him 100%.

Sean mopes around backyard. Mr. Granger, Tom's grandfather, from next door inquires — haven't seen you and Tom lately. Sean says Tom always said friends are friends in bad times as well as good, but then Tom abandoned him for the "cool" kids. What makes kids cool? Sean says Mr. Granger wouldn't understand. He just has to know that he, Sean, isn't cool. Mr. Granger disagrees. Anyway, that's not what's bugging Sean — it's the park. Mr. Granger knows the park — it's the heart and lungs of the city. He urges Sean to do something about it. Sean doesn't want to — a kid doesn't have any say-so in city affairs. Granger reminds him the park was a friend to him — he should be a friend to it. What can he do? Old man tells him to go to the meeting with as much community support as he can get.

Sean sends out an email blast to the group. They need to meet in their spot ASAP.

Kathy is the last to arrive for an emergency meeting of the Bike Squad. Sean outlines goal of saving the park and suggests some tactics as Kathy taps out a rhythm with an old set of drumsticks. They all object. Then Sean quotes Spider-Man, Batman, Superman, X-Men. What would they do in a case like this? They finally agree — they'll do a multimedia display: music (especially drums), charts, PowerPoint — a multimedia presentation to the city.

Act 2

They prepare a news release and a pamphlet, and then go door to door to campaign to get neighbors to go to the meeting. Most people don't want to get involved. Some slam the door in their faces. Others can't take time. A few promise sincerely that they'll come.

Ben tells Raffi he wants to help. Raffi turns him down, but Ben blackmails him. Kathy falters; Sean gets her back.

The Bike Squad distributes flyers all over town. Kathy gets separated from the group. A couple of older kids harass her. Tom helps her out of the jam. He escorts her back to the clubhouse. She is smitten.

In the parking lot of Rosebud Electronics, the kids slip flyers under the windshield wipers of cars. The security guard runs them off, takes one of the flyers, reads it. Stone's assistant exits the building to go to lunch. The guard hands her the flyer. She doesn't want to take it, but he insists.

In the offices of Rosebud Electronics, Stone's assistant hands him the flyer the kids are distributing. His assistant says they have a point. He goes into a rage. Can't they see what a factory would do for this town? They can't stop progress. The town will die. Don't they understand that he's doing this for the good of the town? It's how business is done.

At the clubhouse, Kathy tries to get Sean to accept Tom's help. Sean says we don't need his help. Kathy disagrees. Sean says, trust me, he'll only dump out on you when the going gets tough. He's not a true friend. Kathy says why don't you give him another chance? Sean says he had his chances.

Sean and his family have dinner. Sean's father doesn't want him to go to the town meeting, but his mother is all for it. Sean states his case for the park, and the father agrees with the mother: It may not be the best thing, but at least Sean would get a good civics lesson.

Town meeting. Hardly anyone shows up. Mr. Granger is there with Tom. Stone makes his presentation. Very convincing. Beautification, urban renewal, economy, etc. He outlines his plans for a new park on the land the company owns on the outskirts of town. Raffi and Kathy waiver. Sean brings them back. Sean gets up and presents their program. He tells them park users won't go to the suburbs — older people and kids just don't have the transportation. It's a neighborhood park. But the neighbors haven't shown up to support it.

They leave. Tom follows the squad outside. He asks to be let back in to the squad. This is the first time Kathy and Raffi learn he was even in in the first place. They urge Sean to let him in. He was there at the meeting when no one else showed up. Sean relents.

That night, Sean is watching an old movie on his computer when his mother comes into his room. She tells him it's time to turn off the computer and go to sleep. He begs to be able to finish it — it's *The Maltese Falcon*. She relents and then tells him how proud she is of him for what he tried to do.

The next day, while they ride to their meeting place, Tom suggests if they can't sway community, why not try to change Stone? Kathy agrees, but Sean says "Heart of Stone. Ever heard of that? How can they change his mind? It's all about business with this guy."

Tom — Why is park so important to you and not to him?

Sean — Because we have fun there. He doesn't.

Tom — Exactly. He doesn't know how to have fun like we do. Let's get
    him on a bike.

Sean — So we've got to show him how to have fun in park.

Midpoint

Sean and Tom talk before the others arrive for the meeting. Tom wants his grandfather at the meeting. Sean doesn't think that's a good idea, but Tom says his grandfather has a lot of good ideas.

Club meeting — How are they going to get Stone to have fun? To get him to the park? Mr. Granger has an idea. Make a deal with him. They'll drop their opposition if he spends one day at the park with them.

They try to get Stone on the phone. No deal. They try to get into the office. Nope. They try to meet him at his house. Foiled. Finally, they dress as janitors and get inside the building. They present the idea to Stone. He turns them down. Then his assistant points out what good PR it would be. Eventually, Stone agrees.

At the park they take him for a soccer game. He hates soccer. Football, that's a real game. They get him on a skateboard and try to have him glide through the park. He can't balance. They take him on a bike trail. He falls and breaks his arm.

Now he's angry. It's all over. They're going to build the factory here, no matter what.

Sean is angry at Tom and yells at him. It's his fault Stone broke his arm. He was the one who suggested biking. He walks away.

Act 3

At home, Sean is upset. Not only has he ruined the chance to keep the park, but he said some things he didn't even mean to Tom. Sean's dad urges him to tell that to Tom. Sean swallows his pride and goes over to Tom's to apologize. Tom doesn't accept. "Why should I?" But Sean reminds him: Friends are friends in bad times as well as good.

Mr. Granger asks what happened. Sean is reluctant to talk, but Tom explains that they tried, but failed, even though they worked hard at it. Granger realizes that Sean didn't do his research. He only presented what was fun for the Bike Squad. What's fun for Stone? Sean doesn't know. Where's he from? Cleveland. Cold. Snow. Granger asks what people do in that kind of climate. Skiing, skating, sledding, Sean replies. Granger just stands there. "Rosebud Electronics," he says. Sean doesn't understand. Mr. Granger says, "You like old movies, right? Look it up."

Sean at his computer watching *Citizen Kane*. He sees the sled go into the fire at the end. "Rosebud" is the name of the sled. He sends out an email calling for a meeting the next morning.

At the Bike Squad meeting, Sean explains about Rosebud. He says we've got to build a downhill run for a sled. That seems like too much work for the squad, but Tom says he's in. Then Raffi offers to organize a snowmaker. Kathy calculates amount of ice necessary. How are they going to get it there? That's for Sean to figure out. He offers his dad's truck — hoping he can get him to drive it.

At home, after a short battle, Sean convinces his dad to help. He sees how important it is to Sean and doesn't care about the plumbing contract.

With Raffi watching from a hiding place, Ben gives Stone's assistant something. Moments later, Stone finds a photo of a sled in the park on his desk. The assistant claims not to know where it came from.

Sean is at the door of an ice-making company. He pulls some money out of his pocket. The man shakes his head. He tells the man it will be good publicity. The man still doesn't care. He asks the man to take a chance. If it works, he'll be able to pay next year and every year after that.

The process of snow making in the summer. It's tough. It melts. They've got to get Stone there before it's gone. But he's not coming. They find a way to shut down the electricity in his office. His assistant agrees to hide his cell phone. Since he can't work, maybe he can play.

Stone shows up at park. There's a large patch of snow from the top of the hill to the bottom. No footprints in it. And a sled at top of hill. The sled has a sign. Sit on me.

The squad watches from bushes. Stone sits on the sled. Starts to get up, but Sean races out, pushes him down the hill. Scared at first, he tries to stop. Tom, Raffi, Kathy, and Ben push him. Stone laughs, zooms down the hill. Steers with feet. By the bottom of hill, he's laughing hysterically. Picks up sled and runs back to top and does it again. Kids come out. He encourages them to join him. They don't have sleds. He says, improvise. Trash can lids, cardboard, sheets of plastic. Whatever. Soon, the hillside is covered with people having fun — lots of it.

At the building commission, Sean represents the Rosebud Electronics Company as he points out the fine points of the new factory plan — the one that will be built on the company's land on the edge of town. He discusses some recent additions to the drawings: a fun room for break time, a day care center, and a playground for the local kids. He also announces the annual sledding in the summer event at the central park.

. . . . . .

Though the cuts were simple and few, they made the story flow faster. Some cuts were tough. There was some good stuff there. But any lost information was imparted in a line or two in another part of the script instead of a whole scene. Here's what he turned it into (the production company changed the title — a good move).

The Kids Who Saved Summer
Beat Sheet by Martín Olmedo

Sean tears through the kitchen spouting a line from *Star Wars*, grabbing food, whirling as he downs a quick OJ. Mom tries to make him slow down, have a real breakfast. "Mom, please. There's a Bike Squad emergency."

Sean leaves house at a run, putting helmet on. Ignores neighbor boy, Tom, who tries to flag him down. Bikes down the street.

Raffi, in a hurry, feeds himself and his younger brother, Ben, breakfast, fields his nosy questions, then flies out the door, grabbing his helmet. Bikes down the street.

Kathy, in the midst of playing a major drum solo, hears Mom screaming. Stops playing. Mom tells her she promised not to practice more than one hour per day. Time's up. Kathy's reluctant to stop, then realizes she's late. Bikes down the street.

Three cyclists converge — fall in behind Sean. Race to the house where they attempt rescue of a Frisbee. They fail.

They ride through the park on the way to their clubhouse. People enjoying the park, especially seniors and children. Some kids a year or two older play touch football. Kathy notices Tom, asks Sean about him. It's a sore subject — Tom dropped him for his in-group friends. They're in different worlds now.

In their park secret meeting place, there's a debriefing about the Frisbee incident. Ben intrudes. Raffi sends him home.

Construction noise stops their meeting. Workers put up a notice of a conditional use permit meeting. The workers tell them Rosebud

Electronics Company wants to build a factory on the site. Can't be, Sean says. It's public land. Worker says company wants to swap larger plot of land on edge of town. Kathy stops her fidgeting long enough to do a square foot calculation, a tax calculation, a tax credit calculation — the deal makes sense. "They can't do this," Sean says.

Sean argues with his father about the company's plans. But Dad knew about, and is in favor of, the swap. Says the whole Chamber of Commerce is in favor: It's going to be great for urban renewal, increased property values, and taxes to pay for schools. It'll provide for jobs in a depressed economy. Good for everyone, especially him — he'll supply plumbing fixtures. Sean's POV — kids need a place to have fun. Family place. Why can't they have a factory out of town?

Frederic Stone, the president and CEO of Rosebud Electronics, makes a presentation to the Chamber of Commerce. When objections are brought up, he says if it's too much hassle, he'll just cancel the deal, unload the property, and take his jobs and influx of capital to another, less difficult, town. Sean's father leads the audience in applauding him and assures him they're behind him 100%.

Sean mopes around backyard. Mr. Granger, Tom's grandfather from next door, inquires — haven't seen you and Tom lately. Sean says Tom always said friends are friends in bad times as well as good, but then Tom abandoned him for the "cool" kids. What makes kids cool? Sean says Mr. Granger wouldn't understand. He just has to know that he, Sean, isn't cool. Mr. Granger disagrees. Anyway, that's not what's bugging Sean — it's the park. Mr. Granger knows the park — it's the heart and lungs of the city. He urges Sean to do something about it. Sean doesn't want to — a kid doesn't have any say so in city affairs. Granger reminds him the park was a friend to him — he should be a friend to it. What can he do? Old man tells him to go to the meeting with as much community support as he can get.

Kathy is the last to arrive for an emergency meeting of the Bike Squad. Sean outlines goal of saving the park and suggests some tactics as Kathy taps out a rhythm with an old set of drumsticks. They all object. Then Sean quotes Spider-Man, Batman, Superman, X-Men. What would they do in a case like this? They finally agree — they'll do a multimedia display: music (especially drums), charts, PowerPoint — a multimedia presentation to the city.

Act 2

They prepare a news release and a pamphlet, then go door to door to campaign to get neighbors to go to the meeting. Most people don't want to get involved. Some slam the door in their faces. Others can't take time. A few promise sincerely that they'll come.

The Bike Squad distributes flyers all over town. Kathy gets separated from the group. A couple of older kids harass her. Tom helps her out of the jam. He escorts her back to the clubhouse. She is smitten.

In the offices of Rosebud Electronics, Stone's assistant hands him the flyer the kids are distributing. His assistant says they have a point. He goes into a rage. Can't they see what a factory would do for this town? They can't stop progress. The town will die. Don't they understand that he's doing this for the good of the town? It's how business is done.

At the clubhouse, Kathy tries to get Sean to accept Tom's help. Sean says we don't need his help. Kathy disagrees. Sean says, trust me, he'll only dump out on you when the going gets tough. He's not a true friend. Kathy says why don't you give him another chance? Sean says he had his chances.

Town meeting. Hardly anyone shows up. Mr. Granger is there with Tom. Stone makes his presentation. Very convincing. Beautification, urban renewal, economy, etc. He outlines his plans for a new park on the land the company owns on the outskirts of town. Raffi and Kathy waiver. Sean brings them back. Sean gets up and presents their program. He tells them park users won't go to the suburbs — older people and kids just don't have the transportation. It's a neighborhood park. But the neighbors haven't shown up to support it.

They leave. Tom follows the squad outside. He asks to be let back in to the squad. This is the first time Kathy and Raffi learn he was even in in the first place. They urge Sean to let him in. He was there at the meeting when no one else showed up. Sean relents.

While they ride to their meeting place, Tom suggests if they can't sway community, why not try to change Stone? Kathy agrees, but Sean says "Heart of Stone. Ever heard of that? How can they change his mind? It's all about business with this guy."

Tom — Why is park so important to you and not to him?

Sean — Because we have fun there. He doesn't.

Tom — Exactly. He doesn't know how to have fun like we do. Let's get him on a bike.

Sean — So we've got to show him how to have fun in the park.

Midpoint

Club meeting — How are they going to get Stone to have fun? To get him to the park? Then Sean has an idea. Make a deal with him. They'll drop their opposition if he spends one day at the park with them.

They try to get Stone on the phone. No deal. They try to get into the office. Nope. They try to meet him at his house. Foiled. Finally, they dress as janitors and get inside the building. They present the idea to Stone. He turns them down. Then his assistant points out what good PR it would be. Eventually, Stone agrees.

At the park they take him for a soccer game. He hates soccer. Football, that's a real game. They get him on a skateboard and try to have him glide through the park. He can't balance. They take him on a bike trail. He falls and breaks his arm.

Now he's angry. It's all over. They're going to build the factory here, no matter what.

Sean is angry at Tom and yells at him. It's his fault Stone broke his arm. He was the one who suggested biking. He walks away.

Act 3

At home, Sean is upset. Not only has he ruined the chance to keep the park, but he said some things he didn't even mean to Tom. Sean's dad urges him to tell that to Tom. Sean swallows his pride and goes over to Tom's to apologize. Tom doesn't accept. "Why should I?" But Sean reminds him: Friends are friends in bad times as well as good.

Mr. Granger asks what happened. Sean is reluctant to talk, but Tom explains that they tried, but failed, even though they worked hard at it. Granger realizes that Sean didn't do his research. He only presented what was fun for the Bike Squad. What's fun for Stone? Sean doesn't know. Where's he from? Cleveland. Cold. Snow. Granger asks what people do in that kind of climate. Skiing, skating, sledding, Sean replies. Granger just stands there. "Rosebud Electronics" he says. "Rosebud." The light comes on in Sean's brain.

"Rosebud!" Sean says. "I should have known that from *Citizen Kane*. It's the name of Kane's sled. He needs to go sledding in the park."

At a Bike Squad meeting, Raffi organizes snowmaker. Kathy calculates amount of ice necessary. How are they going to get it there? That's for

Sean to figure out. He offers his dad's truck — hoping he can get him to drive it. At home, after a short battle, Sean convinces his dad to help. He sees how important it is to Sean and doesn't care about the plumbing contract.

With Raffi watching from a hiding place, Ben gives Stone's assistant something. Moments later, Stone finds a photo of a sled in the park on his desk. The assistant claims not to know where it came from.

The process of snowmaking in the summer. It's tough. It melts. They've got to get Stone there before it's gone. But he's not coming. They find a way to shut down the electricity in his office. Since he can't work, maybe he can play.

Stone shows up at park. There's a large patch of snow from the top of the hill to the bottom. No footprints in it. And a sled at top of hill. The sled has a sign. Sit on me.

The squad watches from bushes. Stone sits on the sled. Starts to get up, but Sean races out, pushes him down the hill. Scared at first, he tries to stop. Tom, Raffi, Kathy, and Ben push him. Stone laughs, zooms down the hill. Steers with feet. By the bottom of hill, he's laughing hysterically. Picks up sled and runs back to top and does it again. Kids come out. He encourages them to join him. They don't have sleds. He says, improvise. Trash can lids, cardboard, sheets of plastic. Whatever. Soon, the hillside is covered with people having fun — lots of it.

At the building commission, Sean represents the Rosebud Electronics Company as he points out the fine points of the new factory plan — the one that will be built on the company's land on the edge of town. He discusses some recent additions to the drawings: a fun room for break time, a day care center, and a playground for the local kids. He also announces the annual sledding in the summer event at the central park.

Cutting Down Scenes

This is getting bloody, but soon it's going to go to the bone, so take a deep breath. Let's say that what remains after the slaughter of the 10% are scenes crucial to the storytelling of your movie. Fine. Now let's cut down each individual scene by 10%. You're kidding, right? No. You really need to tighten up each scene.

How to do that? Remember when we were talking about the structure of scenes and we said that it's a good idea to enter as late as possible and leave as soon as you've accomplished your goal for the scene? You can enter even later and leave even earlier.

First of all, it's sometimes not necessary to show the ordinary life segment of the scene, especially if we've been in this place or with these people before. We already know what their ordinary life is going to be. So you may, as long as it's not confusing, start with what the Spanish call the *detonante* of the scene. The detonator. We call it the inciting incident. It's what kicks off the action of the scene and propels it. It's what makes the need of the protagonist of the scene come alive.

In some cases, you can start even after that, so long as we understand what that need is and what the protagonist's drive is by inferring something from the previous scene.

In the middle of the scene, you can cut down on description, especially specifics regarding the decoration of a room, the foliage of an outdoor place, or whatever gets in the way of the forward action. Certainly take out any camera direction and placement. That's not for you to determine anyway, and it only gets in the way of the reading. Let the director do the job. All you want to do is to enable the reader to visualize the story, not every single shot.

As you approach the end of your scene, try to determine when you've made the point of the scene, and cut out everything that follows that point. That probably will mean you can cut the return to normal life at the end of the scene. You can sometimes even cut the final challenge of the scene if we can predict the outcome from what we've learned about the characters or from what we're about to see in the next scene.

For example, let's say that you've established that the quiet, self-effacing character played by Jackie Chan will do everything in his power not to fight an enemy, unless provoked by a reference to his mother. Let's say the scene points are these:

1. Ordinary life: He enters a restaurant and the host shows him to a table for four. He asks about the others. They haven't arrived.

2 The inciting incident: The waiter comes to the table and tells him someone wants to see him in the alley. He declines to go.

3. End of act 1: The waiter returns with a note signed by his mother — it's extremely urgent he come to the alley. Reluctantly, he decides to go.

4. Midpoint: As he enters the alley, he's jumped by three men. He realizes he was naïve and made a mistake. They tackle him to the ground and …

5. Low point: … beat him. It looks like he'll never get out of this alive.

6. Final challenge: He sees his mother lying in a doorway, her hands and feet bound. It gives him more motivation as she must really be in trouble. He fights off the men.

7. He walks down the street with a black eye, but he has his mother by his side.

How could we cut this down? We could start at the inciting incident, leaving readers to assume how he got to the restaurant table. He gets the note and immediately goes to the alley despite his suspicions. Do we need to see the fight? It's a Jackie Chan movie, so, yes, it's all about the fight. However, let's say a not-so-elegant actor is playing the role and it's not a martial arts movie; then we could cut from the challenge to the next scene where he's walking down the street with his mother and his black eye. We get the picture.

To Do

Choose a ten-page excerpt from your script that you think is pretty tight already. Now, cut a page from it. Use any tricks you can think of, but get it down to nine pages. Then come back here.

You see, it *was* possible.

Cutting Dialogue

How do you cut dialogue without cutting information that is essential to the story? First of all, you make sure that you must absolutely have to have that information in dialogue. It's probably more effective to see in action. Action is quicker. They're called *motion* pictures, and if you can move your story forward with moving pictures only, you'll make more of an impression on your audience than if you rely entirely on words (dialogue). If you illuminate your character by a physical attribute or something he does, it's always better than telling about it in dialogue.

Then, assuming you've changed any dialogue to action that you could, are all the remaining words necessary? Quite often, you'll find that characters go through a little "throat clearing" at the beginning of their speeches. Sometimes, that can be a good character trait. But mostly it's not. It's a waste of reader's time, just like, "Hello. How are you?" would be. Or even a "Goodbye" on the telephone. If they waste time, if they're not absolutely needed, then they're out.

Then you'll need to make sure each word of dialogue is authentic to that character. Would he really say those lines, those words? Would a street tough call a rival "effete"?

While you're doing this, you can make sure the dialogue conveys character. That means we can learn something from the way he says something as much as from what he says. For example, what's the difference between "Busy as hell" and "Busier than a one-armed paper hanger"?

One last question: Could another character have said that sentence? If so, then it's probably not in character. That means you'll either have to change the language to suit the character or reassign the line to another.

Then cut dialogue that's unnecessary because you've already told the reader or the audience that information in another way. Often, you'll have one character tell another character something he doesn't know, but the reader knows because she's read it earlier. In that case, cut deeper into the scene. Sometimes you'll write something in description that a character then describes in dialogue. Cut one or the other. Preferably the dialogue.

To Do

Read the following pages. Cut them from eight pages to six pages by eliminating wasteful, repetitious, or character-inappropriate dialogue. Cut descriptive lines that aren't needed or don't move the action. Be brutal. This scene definitely needs help!

```
FADE IN:

INT. R & J'S APARTMENT - EVENING

We can hear the wail of an infant who wants her
dinner. We can also hear the grunts and groans and
the moans and heavy breathing of a pair of people
having sex. As the camera tours the living room,
we can see what a shambles it's in, with cloth-
ing strewn everywhere, dirty dishes on top of dirty
dishes on top of newspapers and magazines. The
television is on in the corner. The windows have
baby handprints on them. The floor is a mess.

We follow the moans and groans to one of the bed-
rooms and find JULIET, 19, pretty, long, dark hair,
receiving VICENTE, 21. They're enjoying this a lot,
```

but Juliet's concerned. She's afraid Romeo's going
to be coming home soon and she wants Vicente out as
soon as possible. She's putting everything she can
into the effort to finish quickly.

> JULIET
> Yes, yes. Come on, Vinnie.
> Come on, boy.

> VICENTE
> (breathing hard, he's
> thinking she really likes
> him)
> Juliet, Juliet, I... I... I
> love you. I'm going to...
> I'm going to...

LOUD DOOR KNOCKS

Vicente suddenly stops. He looks towards the door.

> VICENTE
> What's that?

> ROMEO (OS)
> Julie! Come on. Open up.
> I'm hungry.

> JULIET
> Oh, no. It's my husband!
> Hurry up! You have to go.

> VICENTE
> I'm almost finished.

She pushes him off and jumps out of bed. She dresses
quickly as she talks. He just sits there at first
trying to figure out what happened. She tells him to
get moving.

> JULIET
>
> You are finished. We're
> both finished if you don't
> get out of here. Hurry up
> and get dressed. I'll stall
> him while you go out the
> window.

> VICENTE
>
> What? It's two stories
> down, girl. What am I,
> Superman?

> JULIET
>
> You said you were a couple
> of minutes ago.

> VICENTE
>
> And that was like, that was
> like what I felt, but, like
> I said, it was really that
> I meant you make me feel
> like Superman. Why can't
> you stay a little while
> longer?

> JULIET
>
> Because Romeo will be
> pissed off that his
> dinner's not on the table
> and that little Romeo's
> crying.

> VICENTE
>
> Why don't you let me talk
> to him to see if--

> JULIET
>
> Are you out of your mind?
> Get out of here, now. Take
> the fire escape. Hurry up
> before he bursts in here.

> VICENTE
>
> Okay, if you're so worried.
> I'll do it.

He gets up to hug her but she's already dressed
and goes out into the hallway, shutting the door
behind her.

INT. R & J'S APARTMENT - EVENING

The knocking continues on the door as Juliet walks
through the messy living room. She goes to the
door, which had a chain on it and a deadbolt.

> JULIET
>
> Who is it?

          ROMEO (OS)
        (through the door)
       Julie, who the hell do you
       think it is? It's your
       husband home for dinner,
       and it had better be good.
       Open the damn door. What's
       the matter with you?

She unlocks the door, undoes the chain, and ROMEO,
20, storms in. He's wearing black pants, a white
shirt with a loosened black tie, and a green
apron. He has a name tag on his shirt that says,
"I'm Romeo. Ask me about the produce here."

          ROMEO
       Jeez, what a sty. What have
       you been doing all day?
        (on hearing baby
         Romeo crying)
       Is that the baby? What the
       hell's going on here? Why
       did you have the door
       locked like that?

          JULIET
       There have been some break-ins.
       I didn't feel safe.

There's a crash that sounds like it came from the
bedroom.

> ROMEO
> What the...

He runs down the hall and into the

INT. R & J'S APARTMENT (BEDROOM) - EVENING

Romeo enters running and finds baby Romeo crawling on his hands and knees, a lamp broken into little pieces lying on the floor.

> ROMEO
> Juliet! Get your sorry ass
> in here.

> JULIET
> Romeo, I can explain. It's
> just that I've been so
> lone--

But she stops as she enters the room and sees it's just baby Romeo and the lamp. She also notices that the bed has been made and the window to the fire escape is still open, the curtain flowing in the breeze.

> ROMEO
> You've been what?

> JULIET
> I've been lonesome without
> you, honey.

She tries to throw her arms around his neck, but he won't have any of it.

```
                    ROMEO
                 (angry)
              Clean this mess up, will
              you, before Baby Romy gets
              hurt. I'm going to take a
              shower. I had to work in
              the parking lot half the
              day. And I get home and the
              house is a mess, the kid is
              out of control, and there's
              no food. Dinner better be
              on the table when I get
              out.
```

Now, before you read on, do the exercise. Best way to do this is to photocopy these pages (and these pages only, of course), then mark them up. Then come back here to see another way to do it.

Okay, it was tough, right? But not impossible. Here's how I might do it:

```
FADE IN:

INT. R & J'S APARTMENT - EVENING

An infant WAILS.

GRUNTS and GROANS of people having sex.

The living room is in a shambles — clothing strewn
everywhere, dirty dishes on top of newspapers and
magazines.

IN THE BEDROOM
```

JULIET, 19, long, dark hair, receives VICENTE,
21. Juliet's putting everything she can into the
effort.

> JULIET
> Yes, yes. Come on, Vinnie.
> Come on, boy.

> VICENTE
> Juliet, Juliet, I... I... I
> love you. I'm going to...
> I'm going to...

LOUD DOOR KNOCKS

Vicente suddenly stops. He looks towards the door.

> VICENTE
> What's that?

> JULIET
> Oh, no. It's Romeo.
> You have to get out
> of here.

> VICENTE
> I'm almost finished.

She pushes him off, jumps out of bed.

> JULIET
> You are finished.

She dresses quickly.

(Cont'd)

                    JULIET

We're both finished
if you don't get
out of here. Hurry up
and get dressed. I'll
stall him while you
go out the window.

                    VICENTE

What? It's two stories
down, girl. What am I,
Superman?

                    JULIET

You said you were a
couple of minutes ago.

                    VICENTE

I meant, like, you make
me feel like Superman,
you know? Why don't you
let me talk to him. See if--

                    JULIET

Are you out of your
mind? Get out of here.
Take the fire escape.
Hurry!

He gets up to hug her, but she's already moving out
of the room. She shuts the door behind her.

INT. R & J'S APARTMENT - EVENING

The knocking continues. Juliet reaches the door,
which has a deadbolt and chain.

> JULIET
> Who is it?

> ROMEO (O.S.)
> (through the door)
> Who the hell do you
> think it is? Open
> the damn door.

She unlocks the door, undoes the chain, and ROMEO,
20, storms in. He wears black pants, a white shirt
with a loosened black tie, and a green apron. His
name tag says, "I'm Romeo. Ask me about the produce
here."

The baby CRIES.

> ROMEO
> What the hell's going
> on here? Why did you
> have the door locked
> like that?

> JULIET
> There have been some
> break-ins. I didn't
> feel safe.

There's a crash that sounds like it came from the
bedroom.

                    ROMEO
          What the...

He runs down the hall and into the

THE BEDROOM.

Romeo enters running and finds baby Romeo crawling
on his hands and knees, a lamp broken into little
pieces lying on the floor.

                    ROMEO
          Juliet! Get your sorry
          ass in here.

                    JULIET (O.S.)
          Romeo, I can explain.
          It's just that I've been
          so lone--

But she stops as she enters the room and sees it's
just baby Romeo and the lamp. The bed has been made
and the window to the fire escape is still open.

                    ROMEO
          You been what?

                    JULIET
          I've been lonesome
          without you, honey.

She tries to throw her arms around his neck, but he
won't have any of it.

```
          ROMEO
        (angry)
     Clean this shit up
     before Baby Romy
     gets hurt. I'm going
     to take a shower.
     Dinner better be on
     the table when I get
     out.
```

To Do

Now take a scene from your own script and pare it down to its bare minimum. Be just as brutal.

Not much left to go. The hard part is over for this draft. How about giving yourself a pat on the back? Arm not long enough? How about taking yourself and someone you like out to dinner? Better yet, how about letting that person take you out? Then apply your butt to the chair again and finish up.

WHERE AM I?

I congratulate you. First of all, you have read this far. Second, you may have already completed your rewrite. But now it's time to take your script's temperature and see if you can take it off intensive care. It's time to do a script status report (SSR).

The purpose of the SSR is to know truly where you are, at least in your own estimation, before you start making "I'm finished!" noises. Here's an opportunity to develop some distance from your script. Objectivity is hard to achieve, but, for the moment, pretend that someone else wrote your script, then read it again. Yep. Again. And, as usual, I'll wait until you're done.

Back already? Fast reader. Okay, now it's time to see how objective you really are. Please fill out the following as honestly as possible.

Script Status Report

Project name:

What is the premise of your script in one sentence (theme or idea, not story)?

Who is the main character in one sentence?

What does he think he wants at the end of the first act? What does he really want at the midpoint?

What inside of him is preventing him from achieving that?

Who or what is preventing him from achieving that? (Who is the antagonist?)

What does he have to learn about himself (his flaw)?

Who are the other main players, including the antagonist and the person who is the central emotional relationship? What are their needs?

What is the genre of your script?

What is the everyday life of the protagonist?

What is the inciting incident?

What is the act 1 goal and plan?

What is the midpoint?

What is the act 2 curtain (the low point)?

What is the final challenge?

What is the return to the (now changed forever) normal life?

What is working?

What is not working?

What must change?

Happy with what you read? Good. Go to the next chapter.

Not so happy? Okay. Not unusual. Remember how many drafts I told you some writers go through? You may have a few drafts to go. For now, go back and really work on "what is not working?" When you're satisfied that the script represents the best that you can do, go to the next chapter.

THE RIGHT LOOK

You've read my comments earlier about there being no rules in screenplay writing, just guidelines. If you follow the guidelines, you'll have a script that reads and looks professional. But that doesn't necessarily guarantee a great, or even good, script. There are many times when it's a good idea to go outside of convention, to surprise your reader in both form and content.

Shane Black, for example, went outside of the rules in *Lethal Weapon* when he talked directly to the reader, addressing them as "boys and girls" and "folks." He even describes a posh Beverly Hills house as "the kind of house I'll buy if this movie is a big hit." Thousands of neophyte screenwriters have copied that technique in spec scripts ever since, to the point at which it's no longer fresh, much less unique, and considered by many to be just plain derivative. He became a parody of his own style with *Kiss Kiss, Bang Bang* when he talked to the audience in narration. But when he first did it, it suddenly engaged a reader like never before.

If you do it, you'll get slammed. You're not Shane Black. But you can still color outside the lines for effect, so long as you don't overdo it. You need to know where the lines are first. I suggest you have a look at *A Practical Guide to Flawless Screenplay Form*, by Janna E. Gelfand (Get It Right Press) or *The Screenwriter's Manual: A Complete Reference of Format and Style*, by Stephen E. Bowles, Ronald Mangravite, and Peter A. Zorn Jr. (Pearson). Know the conventions, but don't be afraid to blow them off for effect or to improve the flow of your story.

Robert Downey Jr., Kiss Kiss, Bang Bang, *written and directed by Shane Black (Warner Bros. and Silver Pictures, 2005).*

For example, separate slug lines within a scene can really slow down the reader. It's true that you should write a new scene line or slug line for every change of time or place, but sometimes that just distracts from the story. And while a script is both a technical document (like architectural blueprints), it's also a vehicle for the imagination, like an architectural rendering. So, for example, say we're back in the apartment with Romeo and Juliet. We can establish that time and place with the initial slug line for the scene:

```
INT. R&J'S APARTMENT - DAY
```

But if we move from the living room to the hallway to the bedroom, we can assume the reader is going to know where we are and just use a few words to tell us where we're going:

```
Romeo stomps down the
HALLWAY
And tramps into the
BEDROOM
Where he sees Baby Romeo playing on the floor with a
broken lamp.
```

Technically, he's moved from one set to another, so normally we'd have a separate slug line for each room, but let's allow the director to make the decision about how it's shot (and he could have it all pre-lit and shoot it in one smooth take or he could have a series of shots — his call). Right now, what we're interested in is the speed with which the story moves.

Another way to make your story flow faster is to remove "CUT TO" and "DISSOLVE TO." Why? Because every change of scene is at least a cut. If it's anything more than that, let the editor and the director work on it. If you're trying to show passage of time, you could use "DISSOLVE TO," but you'd be better off just showing how time passed by indicating it in the visual — cigarettes butts where there were none, half-finished food on plates, various states of dress or undress (whatever is called for in the scene).

To Do

Go through your script and see if there aren't places you can speed up by cutting down on slug lines and removing "CUT TO" and "DISSOLVE TO."

Spling, Gramma, Punkchewayshun, and Cents

It's easy to make mistakes in spelling, grammar, punctuation, and cents. See, I just did it again, and spell-check wouldn't have caught it. However, mistakes tend to bounce a reader out of the story. And you don't want anything to interrupt the flow. If you have several errors on a page, the reader will (rightly) feel that you are unprofessional and that you didn't think it worthy of your time to take care of the details of writing the script. And if you didn't think it worthy of your time, why would it be worthy of her time to read it? It could also simply mean you haven't mastered your craft. If that's the case, why should they read any further, since, if you haven't mastered the basics, they have no reason to believe you've mastered the hard stuff like characterization and storytelling?

"Yeah, but that's the small stuff, and I don't sweat the small stuff."

Sure, that's an attitude you could reasonably have. After all, the story is what's important, right? The big picture. The heart. The emotion.

And you'd be right to think that. Just as you'd be right to think, when you buy an automobile, it's the engine and the line of the car that are important. Let's say you go into a Mercedes-Benz dealer and want to buy a CL Class coupe, which costs about as much as a high-budget screenplay (somewhere around $120,000). They show you two cars, both brand new: One is in perfect condition, bright and shiny. Not a smudge on it. The other one has several scratches on the door, the tires have been roughed up, there's a tear in the leather seat, the radio is in upside down, and the gearshift knob is cracked.

They both cost the same, but would you buy a new car that's covered in scratches? Why not? It runs, doesn't it? But wouldn't you be suspicious of how it runs? Would you even take the time to take it on a test drive? What if the door handle fell off in your hand? Sure, the salesman could tell you all that could be fixed, but would you really want the ride?

Of course not, because it would be obvious to you that the car company hadn't taken care in the final inspection of the car. So why even bother with a test drive?

Same thing applies to a script. Do your homework. Make it look good. Proofread it. Have a friend (or better yet, a professional) proofread it. Then proofread it again. Make sure you've spelled everything correctly. Make sure that — where you need to be — you are grammatically correct and that the punctuation is correct. But how do you know what is correct?

Use a dictionary. A good one. Check any word that you have any doubt about whatsoever. Use a good grammar book. The one that comes to mind is William Strunk, E. B. White, and Roger Angell's classic *The Elements of Style*. It will help you with both grammar and punctuation.

One more note on punctuation. Why is it so important? Because it helps you clarify your intentions and emphasis. It guides the actor as well as the reader to an interpretation of your text. It sets the rhythm of the character's speech. Look at the following and see if they have different meanings depending on punctuation.

PHILLIP

Why do you want to go there you have it so good here?

PHILLIP

Why? Do you want to go there? You have it so good
here.

PHILLIP

Why do you want to go? There you have it so good.
Here.

PHILLIP

Why do you want to go there? You have it so good
here.

PHILLIP

Why do you want to go? There you have it. So, good.
Here!

And you probably could think of a few more ways to punctuate this very simple sentence. But why leave its interpretation up to the reader? It's your story. Tell the reader what you mean. Don't make her guess.

To Do

Go through your script very carefully and check for spelling, punctuation, and grammar. Remember, you can break grammatical rules if it serves you, and if you do it on purpose. If it's not intentional, you'll just look unprofessional.

Note: The rules don't apply in the same way to dialogue. Your characters should speak with the grammar appropriate to their education, class, and context.

Focusing the Reader's Attention

For some reason, movies today are considered to be a director's medium. If that were truly so, you would be able to hand a director 120 blank pieces of paper, and she would be able to fashion a film from that. Not that I have anything against directors (sometimes I am one myself), but it all stems from the word. Still, they are very protective of their domain, and development executives are enablers in this overprotection, so they don't like to see directing in a script.

How would you direct in a script? By writing camera angles: CLOSE UP, MEDIUM SHOT, TRAVELING SHOT. By writing too much business for an actor (unless it was important for the scene): Charlie swallows his donut, takes another bite and chews. He looks at the donut, shakes his head, and takes another bite. Then he chews some more.

All you really need to say is Charlie eats a doughnut while he listens to Betty. The director and the actor will fill in the rest.

But there are times when it's necessary to know how carefully Charlie chews his donut, in which case, you may specify. There are even more cases when what the reader focuses on in the scene is important to you. That's when you'd just love to use CLOSE UP, or MEDIUM SHOT, or even POV (which some people still use). How to do that without doing that? How to focus a reader without seeming to step on the director or cinematographer's feet? How about this scene:

INT. CAFETERIA - DAY

The place is jammed with college students, mostly FEMALE, mostly provocatively dressed.

```
JESSIE
A nineteen-year-old vixen, wears a short top and pants
riding as low as her anatomy will allow. She reaches for
her
PHONE
Puts it to her ear.

                    JESSIE
          Name dial. Tiffany. Yes.

PHONE RING
But it sounds like an elevator gong. And it's directly
across the table.

TIFFANY
A slovenly girl dressed in black, pulls her phone from
her book bag.

                    TIFFANY
          What?
```

Do you see how we moved the reader's imagination from a wide shot of the cafeteria to a close up of Jessie to an extreme close-up of her phone, to a close shot of Tiffany? We did this by calling out in caps and setting on its own line the important thing we wanted the reader to focus on.

To Do

Go through your script (again!) and cull out the camera directions. Decide what you want the reader to see in each scene and call out the individual shots. Don't overdo it, as that will lengthen your screenplay and become tiresome. Just do it enough to give it a visual pop.

Pacing

Much has been said by screenwriting teachers and authors of screen-writing books about pacing. Some writers relentlessly turn up the juice page after page, creating a pace that is wearing on the reader. Others have no concept or control of pacing so that their scripts are great antidotes to sleepless nights. My view on pacing is that there must be ups and downs from scene to scene, sequence to sequence, with, of course, rising action, moments of frenetic action, and moments of rest.

First of all, what is rising action?

The concept is clear enough — things must get more and more difficult for your protagonist. The action (of whatever kind, martial combat or marital combat) must get progressively more intense as your movie develops. If you have the toughest battle in the first act, where do you go from there? If you maintain the same level of intensity throughout, without turning up the gas, how do you expect a reader/viewer to maintain interest? You must save your biggest, baddest battle for the final challenge, and you must work your way up to that.

But there are important events, battles if you will, along the way. And, sometimes, you must give your reader a little respite after the most intense scenes. There, you should slow down the action a little, let the reader catch her breath, throw in some comic relief (there's a reason for the 2,500-year-old tradition of comic relief), and just rest.

Then pick up the pace just as the reader is lulled into a false sense of security.

To Do

Check the pacing of your story. If you could graph it, it would look like a series of mountain peaks with sharp falloffs and gradual rises to the next peak. Is that how it feels to you when you read it?

FINISHING

When is a script ready? Michael Colleary, co-writer with Mike Werb of *Face/Off*, answers this question by saying, "When you acknowledge it's never going to be done. When it's been proofread. When it looks like it's been written by a professional writer."

Robin Schiff says, "When I've run out of something to do."

Ron Bass says, "When I decide it's the right time to go out, it is the right time to go out."

In other words, you know when you know, according to them. But what about you? They have years of experience and lots of people to review their scripts to get feedback before they release it to their agents or studios, even when they're on assignment. So what should you do if you haven't yet developed a cadre of trusted advisers?

Develop one.

As soon as possible. I've mentioned this before — that they should know something about writing, that they should be able to help you solve problems, and that they *not* be parents, friends, or significant others. If you join a writers' group on the ground or online, you should be able to meet a few writers of similar or more experience that would be willing to trade a read for a read. That means you have to be willing to do the same, but that's a good thing. You can always learn from reading, whether it's a good script or a bad one.

Let's say you're ready now to send your child out into the Arctic winter. I mean, you're ready to send your script out to an agent or a producer. I'm asking you to give it one more read before you do. Actually, I'm asking you to give it eight quick reads. These don't have to be complete reads, as you'll see by the list, because you will be reading for different things each time. In fact, you might even call these reads "passes," as you'll be passing through the script quickly looking at very specific issues.

To Do

1. Read for structure. Make sure your seven points (see chapter 1) are fully realized and balanced in terms of page length. Make sure your scenes have a beginning, middle, and end.

2. Make sure the scenes have conflict and that they move the story forward. Cut any scenes that don't.

3. Read your descriptive paragraphs again. Are they terse? Do they move the story? Do they tell the story in images? Are they grammatically correct when they need to be?

4. There are three separate reads for dialogue. In each, you should ask yourself if you can show it rather than say it. In other words, could your characters be doing something instead of talking about it? Then you'll ask if each word — I mean each "a" and "the" — is necessary. The first dialogue pass is for the main character. Read each of his speeches and only his speeches. Are they consistent in voice? Could another character have said those words? Does his voice stand out from the crowd?

5. Do the same for the antagonist.

6. Do the same for the supporting characters.

7. Go over the whole script one more time and look for cuts. Delete any nonessential scenes, cut heads and tails off of scenes if possible, cut down dialogue whenever possible.

8. And do the final spelling, punctuation, grammar, and sense pass.

One More Thing

I know you're about to kill me. "How many times do I have to revise this thing?" you're probably saying to yourself. A professional writer might revise a script thirty times and, still, when she hands it to a producer, the producer finds something more to change. In fact, a script isn't done until the final cut is made, and it goes into wide release. Even then, some writers would like to do more. But there are just two more areas to look at, and that's it.

It's often said that the first five pages are the most important pages in the script. This is true because they are the pages that engage the reader. Translated to film, they are the first five minutes of the film. And don't you usually make up your mind if you're going to enjoy a film by the first five minutes? Don't you get sucked in or left out by that time?

So you have to polish and polish your first five minutes until they're diamond-like. They have to be engaging in style and story, and they have to introduce your character so that she's likable or fascinating. You have to make your reader want to spend two hours in the dark with these people.

The last five pages are the most important five pages in the script. Wait a second, didn't I just say the first five pages were the most important? Yes, I did. But I've learned to live with this contradiction in my mind because I know it to be true. The last five pages are the most important because they must create a lasting memory for the audience (or reader) as they leave the theater or finish the read. They are what the audience is going to talk about over coffee or martinis later that night or at the water cooler the next day. You want them to have something to think about or something to say about the final challenge. You want to work your film so that the closing visual makes such an impact that the viewer can't wait to tell others about your story.

To Do

Read the first five and the last five pages over. Are these pages the absolute best you can do? If you're not sure, make them better. If you're sure, now's the time to send out your script.

But first, register it with the Writer's Guild of America West Registry, online at *www.wgawregistry.org*. Now you can send it out.

Okay, ONE MORE THING. Read over the script status report you completed earlier. Have you dealt with all the issues you described then? If not, refer to the table of contents for help with those areas. Rewrite what you need to rewrite. Then you're done.

To Whom?

Now comes the hard part — selling the pile of paper you've put all those ink marks on. So, to whom do you give it now?

To answer that, you might start with Kathie Fong Yoneda's book, *The Script Selling Game, A Hollywood Insider's Look at Getting Your Script Sold and Produced* (Michael Wiese Productions), or my former agent's book, *Mind Your Business: A Hollywood Literary Agent's Guide to Your Writing Career*, by Michele Wallerstein (also Michael Wiese Productions). You might start with a list of franchised agents available from the Writers Guild of America, West on its website, *www.wga.org*. You might just ask around, using your network of writers. You might ask your Uncle Harry (who knows, maybe he knows the assistant to the valet at the restaurant where Brad Pitt's agent's assistant likes to get late-night snacks). But whatever you do, don't let it sit in your desk drawer. You've written a script because you had a story to tell. You can't tell your story unless someone reads it. So get someone to read it. Anyone. And ask everyone you know if they know someone else who will read it, preferably someone with some connection to the film business.

Then, if all goes well and the stars are in alignment, a producer will buy it. And ask for a rewrite.

At least you'll know where to start.

And you'll be ready.

But before you start on the next draft, celebrate this one. It was probably more work than you anticipated, but it's much better, isn't it? So reward yourself big time. It was a big job and you deserve something commensurate. A weekend away with nothing to do (it may be hard to do, but force yourself). Just relax, recharge, reinvigorate. Enjoy. That's part of the process, too.

APPLYING REWRITE
TECHNIQUES TO WEBISODES,
TELEVISION, COMICS,
GRAPHIC NOVELS, GAMES,
AND OTHER MEDIA
YET TO BE DEVISED

If there is one constant in the world of entertainment, it's that there will be technological change that we can't predict. I used to say I had done everything in television except put the iron oxide on the tape, but we don't use tape anymore. DVDs have turned into downloads or streaming video; CDs have turned into MP3s. Episodes have turned into webisodes. But what still survives, from platform to platform, is storytelling (even in music, but that's another book). And the basics of storytelling remain the same: You've got to have characters that are interesting and a story that is compelling. How do we do that in the new media?

The same way we did it in the old media. People are people and structure is structure, if somewhat condensed or even twisted. The structure that holds true for a full-length film holds true for a scene and then surely holds true for a six-minute webisode. Dialogue is dialogue — sharp, funny, dramatic. Recently I had to read Aristophanes' *The Frogs* for a course in comic dialogue I'm preparing for the Escuela Internacional de Cinema y Televisión (the film school of Cuba). I couldn't help but notice the similarity that its dialogue had with Judd Apatow's more recent films: There were penis jokes and fart jokes right on the first page. Twenty-five hundred years after Aristophanes used them to get his audience in a particular mood, so does Apatow, the writers on *Two and a Half Men*, and the creators of the website *Funny or Die*.

Charlie Sheen and Jon Cryer, Two and a Half Men, *created by Chuck Lorre and Lee Aronsohn (Warner Bros. Television, Chuck Lorre Productions, and The Tannenbaum Company, 2003–).*

If storytelling is similar in all media, so is the rewriting of the stories. The techniques I've discussed in the previous pages all apply to the new storytelling media (if they are used for storytelling). They may be structurally adjusted somewhat to fit new length requirements or new combinations of media (we haven't just invented the concept of multimedia — have you ever been to a Catholic mass, heard that combination of music and words, seen the many-colored light from stained glass windows, and smelled the incense?), but the seven points still apply to most. Let me be clear that there are other ways and formats, but the one I have espoused still works in just about every medium.

Let's start with television, where literally hundreds of hours of credits have shown me — from *Real Stories of the Highway Patrol* reenactments to an Alpha-Bits commercial, to kids movies on Showtime — that structure is what holds the whole thing together. Let's examine how the structure works for a sitcom first.

Sitcom Structure

A typical sitcom has a two-act structure, which can most easily be described as a "problem leading to a bigger problem." Some sitcoms have three acts and occasionally more, depending on the program. No matter how many acts they have, they still usually follow the seven-point structure used in features, sequences of features, and scenes. Those points, with their sitcom equivalents, are these:

1. Ordinary life: This is a moment in which we see the key players engage in a bit of their daily routine, but it usually ends by presenting a problem that the central character of this episode has to overcome. It's typically called the "cold open" or "tease." The end of the tease is really the second point, or the …

2. The inciting incident (the presentation of the problem): This will compel the character to act, eventually.

3. Act 1 in a sitcom begins when the program comes back from the initial break (there is some flexibility here, depending on network policy). Now the character is looking for a solution to the problem. In the early stages of the act, the problems for the B and C story also spring up, but just assume that their course is similar to the A story. Soon, your character decides on a course of action in order to deal with whatever the inciting incident brought up. A plan is part of that. Now your character works towards that until …

4. Midpoint or turning point: In a feature, this occurs in the middle of act two. In a two-act sitcom, this occurs at the end of act 1. This is when the bigger problem arises that takes the action in a sudden and unexpected direction. The goal may change. A new goal may be added, but your character really looks like he's in trouble.

5. When the show comes back from the midpoint break, the central character works to fix the bigger problem, but things go awry, and they will reach a point where it looks like the character will never be able to succeed. That's the low point of the story, and in a sitcom it comes near the end of the second half of the story. In a feature, it's at the end of the second act. As in a film, this low point is usually the result of something the central character did or said, possibly related to his overall flaw.

6. The final challenge: That final test, the final barrier that your character must overcome in order to reach her goal. By the end of the second act your character solves the problem. This is equivalent to the point near the end of the third act in a feature, sometimes called the climax. Then there's usually a commercial break.

7. After the break, there is the tag, wherein the character returns to normal life. There's usually one last laugh, and then credits.

This is only a guideline, of course. Not all sitcoms are structured exactly like this, but you can find this structure in nine out of ten that make it on air (or cable) (or satellite) (or online). For more on sitcom writing, see *Elephant Bucks*, by Sheldon Bull (Michael Wiese Productions).

One-Hour Dramatic Structure

There is almost no such thing as a typical one-hour dramatic show now. Structure depends primarily on the platform. A one-hour show for Showtime or HBO is usually structured very much like a movie, and the seven points can be laid down over the script with ease. Think of each episode as a one-hour movie and you practically can't go wrong.

However, if you're rewriting one of the *CSI* franchises or a *Mad Men* episode or *Justified*, you've got more than three acts to deal with. You can have up to six "acts" as defined by the platform in order to fit in enough commercials to support the program. As a storyteller, you have to make the seven-point structure work for you while adhering to the disparate needs of the network to keep viewers tied to their network through the commercials. That means a rising crisis just before every break, while still staying true to the story. For more information on one-hour structure, see *Writing the TV Drama Series*, 3rd Edition, by Pamela Douglas (Michael Wiese Productions).

Writing the Television Movie

Some people say that the television movie is making a comeback, but it's still true there are limited opportunities in that field and a wide range of requirements. Some are structured in exactly the same way a feature film is. HBO movies, when they make them, usually take that approach. Movies for Lifetime and The Hallmark Channel tend to use the old seven-act movie-of-the-week (MOW) structure — which also follows the seven points. Rewriting them is the same as rewriting a feature; just make sure where and how the network wants the act breaks.

Writing for the Web

Who knows what writing for the Web is? I've seen hundreds of webisodes and a score of formats, from self-contained little stories, to a rant about shoes, to interlocking episodes that, when cut together, form a traditional half-hour sitcom. The Web is still a wild west of ideas and approaches, not to mention production values that range from Grandma's VHS recorder to a Red Epic-X Pro video camera (probably outdated by the time this hits print).

The best of what I have seen, other than some one-off sketches, are series of episodes that range from five to ten minutes and that serialize a story in such a way that they can be cut together to form a full-length feature, as Crackle.com often does, or a sitcom (a number of Web series try to do this). For many, the ultimate goal is to "graduate" to network or cable television, but others find that they can be more profitable putting their work up on iTunes or YouTube. There are no rules; there never were. But the seven points still apply, both within the episode and within a series of, say, six or ten linked together. And rewriting them, often on the set, is a little more on the fly, but the same process can be applied that we've been talking about, so long as time allows.

For more on writing for the Web, consult *Byte-Sized Television*, by Ross Brown (Michael Wiese Productions).

Other Media

Comics and graphic novels tell the story in pictures, as do film and, to a lesser extent, television. It could be argued that they have more freedom in the way they tell a story, and that would be a valid argument. But you could also argue that the structure could be the same (doesn't have to be, but could be). In any case, the approach taken towards rewriting film also applies to these visual media. Even games, the ones with stories, can be structured in this way. But rewriting may be different according to the technical needs of the game or software itself. Consult your employer.

To Do

If you don't already have a Web series idea, try to break down your film script into Web-length episodes, say, ten of ten minutes each. Make sure each has the seven points and that each ends in a cliff-hanger so the viewer will want to see the next one.

APPENDIX

The Seven Points of *Thelma & Louise*

1. **Ordinary life:** Thelma starts off as the repressed housewife to car salesman, district manager, Darryl, a male chauvinist pig if there ever was one. She even has to ask his permission to go away for the weekend with her friend, Louise, a waitress with an attitude and a steady boyfriend.

2. **Inciting incident:** When a stranger takes Thelma outside a country bar to get some air, he tries to rape her, but Louise stops it by putting a bullet through the man's heart.

3. **End of act 1:** Thelma agrees to go to Mexico after she tells Darryl to "go fuck yourself."

4. **Midpoint or turning point:** Thelma has a sexual awakening with J.D., but he also steals their cash. Thelma takes charge, and she and Louise go on a crime spree.

5. **Low point:** Thelma learns that the police know they're going to Mexico. They're doomed.

6. **Final challenge:** Thelma suggests that they don't give up and get caught, that they should keep goin'. They kiss, hold hands, and drive into the canyon.

7. **Return to the now-changed-forever normal life:** Thelma and Louise are dead, but they are free of men for the first time. The implication is that the audience is now changed forever because of their journey.

APPENDIX

The Seven Points of *Ratatouille*

1. **Ordinary life:** Remy lives in a rat camp with his family on a farm where they eat the trash. He has a great sense of smell and loves combining foods. He argues with his father about eating trash as opposed to fresh foods. His father warns him about humans.

2. **Inciting incident:** While in a human kitchen stealing (his flaw) spices, he's discovered. He narrowly escapes with Gusteau's cookbook. The book literally saves his life as a float in the sewer.

3. **End of act 1:** The stream takes him to Paris and Gusteau's restaurant. He rescues the soup that Linguini, recently arrived from the provinces, had ruined, but then is discovered and captured by Linguini who has orders to kill him. Linguini gives him a chance to cook the soup again. Remy could flee, but comes back to cook.

4. **Midpoint:** He makes a special order that everyone likes and changes Linguini's life.

5. **Low point:** After the kitchen is challenged by Anton Ego, Remy lets in his rat family and angers Linguini. This is the CER low. The story low is he's captured by the chef and held to make a new line of foods.

6. **Final challenge:** After Ego arrives at the restaurant, Remy daydreams a vision of Gusteau who tells him he doesn't need to pretend to be anyone other than who he really is. His father enlists his family

to spring Remy from the trap and help in the kitchen after all the regular employees have deserted Linguini. In the final tasting, Ego's response to the ratatouille is a classic demonstration of the power of showing, not telling. The meal is a hit — and Remy is accepted and recognized for who he is by Linguini et al., though the restaurant fails. Still he [Remy] reaches his goal.

7.   **Return to the now-changed-forever normal life:** Now recognized by the sign outside his new restaurant, La Ratatouille, Remy cooks, with Colette's help, and Linguini serves. Ego enjoys his investment in the restaurant.

APPENDIX

The Seven Points, More or Less, of
Pirates of the Caribbean: The Curse of the Black Pearl

Keira Knightley, Pirates of the Caribbean: The Curse of the Black Pearl,
*screen story by Ted Elliott, Terry Rossio, Stuart Beattie, and Jay Wolpert,
screenplay by Ted Elliott and Terry Rossio, directed by*
Gore Verbinski *(Walt Disney Pictures, Jerry Bruckheimer Productions, 2003).*

It's hard to say who is the protagonist, Will or Elizabeth. I think it's Elizabeth. Part of the confusion may be due to the number of writers on the project. Jack is definitely the catalyst. Barbossa is the antagonist.

1. **Ordinary life:** Elizabeth's childhood is depicted on the boat to the West Indies somewhere. Will, as a boy, is pulled from the water. She takes his pirate medallion, knowing what it is, to save his life. Her flaw is withholding information from her father. As an adult, she's in denial of her feelings for Will as he is of his feelings for her. She withholds this information from everyone, even herself.

2. **Inciting incident:** Pirates invade. Elizabeth is kidnapped. Will is stunned.

3. **End of act 1 goal:** For Will, to save Elizabeth. For Elizabeth, for Barbossa to leave and never come back.

4. **Midpoint:** Will rescues Elizabeth and escapes. Will's new goal is to bring her back home. Relationship has a moment. Her goal — to return home and be with Will.

5. **Low point:** Will's in the hold. It's flooding. She can't get to him. Pirates seize her again. Monkey has the medallion. Ship blows up. No hope for Will.

6. **Final challenge:** After being freed by the explosion, Will goes to the other ship. Elizabeth saves him. Jack Sparrow fires a shot that saves them all, but it's Will's blood that does it. Then Will saves Jack, then goes free, leaving Will and Elizabeth to their lives.

7. **Return to the now-changed-forever normal life:** Elizabeth saves them again. The rest is presumed.

APPENDIX

Beat Sheet — *In Good Company,* screenplay by Paul Weitz

Ordinary life:

1. Dan Forman goes through the ordinary morning routine and finds out from the news that his magazine has been bought by Teddy K.

2. He also discovers an empty pregnancy test box and thinks his daughter might be pregnant.

3. Dan visits one of his biggest clients, but the client decides to pull his advertising from Dan's magazine.

4. Carter Duryea presents a new marketing strategy for dinosaur phones just as his boss announces he's leaving to head up marketing at the magazine Teddy K has bought. Carter asks to be taken along, and he is.

5. Dan returns home and tries to get his daughter to open up to him (about possible pregnancy).

6. Dan goes to bed, but his wife is up. He asks about his daughter Alex. But his wife tells him she's pregnant. Though he can't believe it at first, he's happy.

7. Carter is excited, but his wife wants him to shut up and go to sleep. She questions his qualifications for the job.

8. Others in Dan's office worry they're going to get fired. Dan gets demoted, his job taken by Carter.

9. Carter and Alex meet in the magazine's elevator. He confesses that he doesn't know what he's doing. She likes that.

Inciting incident sequence:

10. In the office, Dan bumps into Carter by accident. Instead of staying, Dan goes to play tennis with Alex.

11. In an age-versus-youth match, Alex kicks his butt. Then she tells him she's transferring to NYU and will live in the city. Though it's going to be difficult, he agrees to the increased expense.

12. Carter is shown around the office, then shown his office — it's Dan's.

13. Dan returns to find him there. Carter is twenty-six and he's Dan's new boss. Dan responds by throwing a baseball at a trophy after Carter leaves.

14. The nameplates are changed on the office door, and the offices are moved.

15. Carter buys a new Porsche. He immediately gets into an accident.

16. When he gets home, his wife leaves him.

17. At the obstetrician's office, Dan has an attack of arrhythmia and tells his wife, Ann, for the first time that he's been demoted.

18. Carter spends the night in his new car after a fast food meal.

End of act 1:

19. After downing a couple of lattes, Carter has trouble leading a sales meeting. But he comes up with an idea to synergize the sales force and increase sales by 20%. His goal.

Act 2:

Carter takes Dan to a sushi restaurant and forces some sushi on him. He offers him the job of being his "wing man," though Dan doesn't see the merit of that. However, if he takes the position, he'll keep his job.

21. The first man Carter fires is the office kiss-up, who leaves angrily.

22. Carter shows himself to be a lonely workaholic in a series of shots. In one, he puts Dan down at a meeting.

23. Before a meeting, Carter's boss comes and tells Carter he's got to fire some more people. Carter's not happy about it.

24. As the meeting breaks up, Carter desperately tries to get someone to go for a drink with him, but has no takers. Inadvertently, Dan invites him to dinner.

25. Carter is ecstatic to be there, but makes a bad impression on Ann. Dan just wants to get rid of him. Dan and Ann discuss how they're going to meet the new college expenses.

26. Carter meets Alex in the living room. She's somewhat hostile. He admits that it's the anniversary of the first date with his wife. His honesty impresses her.

27. In the kitchen, Ann and Dan argue about Alex at NYU, then Dan drops the ziti on the floor and Ann pukes.

28. Alex and Carter play foosball and talk about peaking too early.

29. The pizza arrives and Dan gets his younger daughter off the phone. Dan calls Alex and Carter, the "kids," in for dinner.

30. At the table, there's some embarrassing conversation, and then Carter spills his drink into Dan's lap. Carter and Alex share a moment.

31. Carter reluctantly leaves, and Alex watches from the window.

32. Alone at his house, Carter feels lonely.

33. Dan helps Alex move to the dorm at NYU.

34. Carter moves to a new apartment in the city.

35. Dan says goodbye to Alex after giving her pepper spray. He struggles to hold back the tears.

36. In matching scenes, Ann and Dan sign mortgage papers while Carter signs divorce papers.

37. Carter forces Dan to take some clients to the corporate box to a concert instead of a game and tells him he has to sell more pages or some people will be let go. They disagree on the use of the term "let go."

38. At the concert, the client is uncomfortable with the atmosphere, but good with Dan. When they sneak out, the client informs him that his mega-corp is feuding with Dan's mega-corp, and he can't do business with him anymore.

39. Carter tells Dan he has to fire Louie and Morty ... or Dan.

40. Dan goes home to his family; Carter sleeps on the couch at work.

41. Dan fires Morty and Louie. They don't take it well.

42. Dan turns in his own evaluation. He doesn't meet expectations.

43. Morty and Louie leave the office. Everyone's sad.

Midpoint:

Carter bumps into Alex at an outdoor café. He has coffee with her. They hit it off and go for a walk.

45. They spend the day and she invites him to her dorm room after kissing him.

46. Alex seduces a reluctant Carter, and he succumbs.

47. In the office the next morning, Dan calls him jumpy, but Carter denies.

48. In a montage, Alex and Carter play tennis, go out for coffee, etc. Carter fires more people. Dan tries calling Alex between shopping trips.

49. In an intramural basketball match, Dan meets Carter's boss, Mark, who's a jerk. There's a ringer on Mark's team. It's a rough game, and Dan gets injured in a dunk attempt.

50. Dan has concerns about getting in touch with his daughter, which Carter allays. Carter asks Dan for advice on keeping a marriage going.

51. Dan's family surprises him with a birthday party. He takes a minute to enter, then comes in wearing only his boxers. Surprise!

52. Dan talks to Morty, who isn't doing well, though his wife got a raise.

53. Carter meets with Alex in his car. He gives her an expensive necklace and tells her she's the kind of girl that it's good to be in a foxhole with (harkening to advice Dan had given him).

54. Later, opening his gifts, Dan discovers that Carter and Alex are together.

Low point:

Dan follows Carter to a restaurant and finds him there with Alex. He slugs him in a confrontation and has words with his daughter.

56. Carter goes to Alex's dorm, but she breaks up with him.

Act 3:

When Dan returns home, he finds that Ann is in the hospital. He goes there, and learns that it was just a scare about the baby.

58. At the hospital, Alex and Dan make up. She tells him he doesn't have to change, but he maintains that he does.

59. At the office, Teddy K shares his vision of the future with everyone. Dan challenges his thinking to his face. Teddy K leaves it to Dan and the others to answer Dan's questions.

60. Mark storms into Dan's office and fires him. Carter resigns, too, but tells him he'll call Teddy K to tell him how Mark's driven the magazine into the ground. They get a short reprieve.

Final challenge:

Dan and Carter visit Mr. Kalb and convince him to make a major ad buy in the magazine.

62. When they return, they find that Teddy K has sold the company to a rival. Mark and Carter lose their jobs, but Dan gets his old one back.

63. As Dan moves back into his office, Carter walks the streets, thinking.

Return to the now-changed-forever normal life:

Carter returns to the office a month later in a sweat suit and goes to see Dan. Carter turns down Dan's offer to come back to work as his second in command, but acknowledges that Dan has done a lot for him. They part with a heartfelt hug.

65. At the elevator, Carter bumps into Alex, who's coming to play tennis with Dan. They have a tense conversation in front of Morty, who reminds them that timing is everything.

66. At the hospital, Dan announces to his daughters that they have a baby sister. He's "psyched."

67. Carter gets a call from Dan while actually jogging outside at the beach. They talk like old friends.

APPENDIX

Alien Abduction
The First Sequence and How It Developed

Alien Abduction, the first "found footage" movie, was shot more than two years before *The Blair Witch Project* and broadcast on UPN, then a fledgling network, now forming part of The CW. The idea was first conceived by Dean Alioto, a writer-director I met while working as coordinating producer on *U.S. Customs Classified*, starring Steven Cannell, in the mid-nineties. Dean had shot a previous version of this using a completely different script (hence the story credit) and had released it to video. He owned it outright. When he came to me at *U.S. Customs Classified* and told me the story, I said, "I can sell that."

I had a brief phone conversation with Neil Stearns at Dick Clark Productions (dcp, then spelled all in small letters). He said, "I can sell that." Dean and I went in to pitch, and we made a deal with them. Dick Clark sat in on the meeting. He loved the idea. In the room, we called it *The McPherson Tape*, but gave it the code name *Country Night* so that no one would guess what we were up to. Later, the network changed it to *Alien Abduction: Incident in Lake County*, which was all right with me.

We then had a roller coaster ride. Showtime bought it in the room, but their business affairs guys couldn't make a deal (in three months!), so we pitched it to Fox, where we were laughed out of the room (I won't say by whom, but he knows who he is). Before we went anywhere else, the guys at dcp sold it internationally, so we were in the black before we sold it to UPN. This time, we brought Dick with us. We pitched it as "War of the Worlds" on video. They literally jumped over the table to shake hands on the deal in a matter of minutes.

I rewrote the story and began the script, always discussing it with Dean. I wanted to make the aliens represent those people we feel alien to us, so there was a sub-theme of racism in the story (the older sister's boyfriend was black and being introduced to the family for the first time). I went through at least twenty drafts from the time it sold until just a week before production when all the brass at UPN were kicked out and new people came in.

They were not thrilled by the original idea: a completely unexplained, found video, shown with no commercial interruptions. Actually, part of that idea had already been abandoned (I wanted it shown without titles or credits, too. Crazy, I know.). But we did convince them to let us shoot it in one take, which we did five times over a period of five days in Vancouver, Canada (again, we wanted to shoot in California, but the tax incentives …).

Once the new guys sent their new VP of development to Vancouver (after threatening to shut it all down after five weeks of preproduction, including the casting of Emmanuelle Chriqui, of *Entourage* fame, as Renee, the girlfriend) to work with me, I went through at least another five drafts in as many days — some more drastic than others. In the end, I counted twenty-seven drafts, not unusual in this business but nerve-wracking when you're producing the picture at the same time.

To make matters worse, once we finished it, they were not thrilled. The foreign distributor was over the moon, though, and they showed the director's cut around the world where it became a cult classic, especially in South America. We still get emails from time to time about how it scared the living daylights out of people.

But UPN wanted it recut to an hour and hired some other people to do it. Fortunately, they didn't change much, just reduced it in length and added another commentary (you can see the difference in style should you ever run across it). Still, it was a blockbuster for UPN, their first MOW and their first one to receive a response on their website (still a relatively new phenomenon). They had more than one million hits overnight the night of the broadcast in their instant poll asking the question, "Do you think this was real or not?"

Viewers split almost evenly, even though there were credits at the end for cast and crew, including "the aliens." Some viewers on sci-fi websites claimed that the credits were government "disinformation" to get us to believe it didn't happen for real. I'm here to tell you that it was a complete fiction.

My purpose in showing you four versions of the first half dozen or so pages is to demonstrate how changes can be large or small and can carry on right onto the set. The last revision I made was on November 2, 1997. We began shooting on the fourth. In the script of record, new dialogue is noted by the script supervisor as actors sometimes improvised (we wished, in the end, they had done that more). So, it's never done until it's broadcast (see above about the recut). Be ready for that.

Here are the first six pages of the first "official" draft. I had written about four drafts before showing it to Dean and another couple before showing it to Neal. Then I called it the first draft.

COUNTRY NIGHT

STORY BY

DEAN ALIOTO

TELEPLAY BY

PAUL CHITLIK

C O N F I D E N T I A L

FOR YOUR EYES ONLY

THIS SCRIPT IS THE PROPERTY OF DICK CLARK FILM GROUP AND MAY NOT BE DISTRIBUTED OR REPRODUCED WITHOUT WRITTEN PERMISSION.

FIRST DRAFT
NOVEMBER 16, 1995

COUNTRY NIGHT

PRODUCTION NOTES

This has got to look and sound like a home video.

We will often hear a person speak before we reach
him/her, but when there's time, the camera will go to
the speaker and follow the conversation. People will
often not wait for the other speaker to finish before
starting to speak themselves. Lots of overlapping
dialogue. And, in places, two or even three people
will be speaking, or yelling, at once.

Camera work will be sometimes jerky, sometimes smooth,
sometimes slow to focus or too dark, sometimes not
looking at anything at all (but not for long) as Tommy
runs or does something that requires his hands.

Swish pans can be just right or way too fast, depending
on the situation and Tommy's level of excitement. The
whole thing should appear as if there are no cuts, as
if shot on one continuous tape, with profanity bleeped,
nudity tiled or blurred in post. The camera never
stops, until the end.

COUNTRY NIGHT

ACT I

DON'T FADE IN:

Just start it cold, close up, right on the face of
TOMMY, 16, who is obviously holding the home video
camera in his hands, looking right into the lens,
trying to figure it out. He pushes it out to arm's
length. We see his hair is short with one side
sculptured. Maybe a gold hoop in one ear. Unbuttoned
long sleeve shirt, t-shirt underneath.

SUPER: In the upper right hand corner of the screen,
the word REC. Just underneath: 0:02:57. The time
will advance in real time throughout.

SUPER: In the lower right hand corner of the screen,
the date: NOV. 23, 1995. The date will remain in the
lower right throughout.

> TOMMY
> Okay, okay. I think I got this
> thing figured out.

> KURT (OS)
> Yeah, right, that's what you've
> been saying for the last half an
> hour.

> TOMMY
> No, the red light's on, this time,
> really.

General cheers and applause from the family...

> TOMMY (Cont'd)
> So, here we go, Thanksgiving at
> the McPherson household.

INT. FARM HOUSE - NIGHT

The camera swings around and focuses on KURT, 25, good
looking, family resemblance to Tommy easy to spot, long
sleeve plaid shirt. Hair a little long, but not
radical. He makes a silly face into the camera as he
sets a large, roasted turkey on the table.

                    TOMMY (OS)
          Nice bird.

                    KURT
          Thank you.

                    TOMMY (OS)
          Like you had anything to do with
          it.

                    KURT
          I paid for it, jerkoff.

                    TOMMY (OS)
          Big whoop.

                    KURT
          You wanna see a bird, I'll show
          you a bird.

Flips him the bird.

                    MOM (OS)
          Come on, boys. Let's not be like
          that tonight.

                    KURT
          Like what?

                    MOM (OS)
          You know like what.

                    TOMMY (OS)
          Mom, aren't we going to wait for
          Melanie and her boyfriend?

The camera gets off Kurt immediately and takes a quick
tour of the dining room...

...until it falls on MOM, 58, holding a bowl of mashed
potatoes.

Following her is LINDA, 25, good looking but a little
worn, doesn't care much how she looks anymore, as she
brings a shallow baking pan to the table.

                    MOM
                (setting down the
                mashed potatoes)
          She'll get here by the time the
          turkey's carved. As usual. Come
          on, everyone, get washed up.
          Tommy, I thought I told you not to
          point that thing at me.

                        TOMMY (OS)
            Come on, Mom, just for a couple of
            minutes. You want your great
            grandchildren to know what you
            looked like, don't you?

She gives him a "I don't care," wave of the hand.

                        TOMMY (OS)
                  (for the camera's
                  benefit)
            That's my mom. The cretin with
            the long hair is my brother, Kurt.
            And the poor woman with the famous
            broccoli casserole is Linda, his
            long suffering wife.

                        KURT
            I'll give you suffering. Go wash
            up like Mom said. Come on,
            everybody. Rosie? Go wash your
            hands, honey.

Camera pans to ROSIE, 6, a cute girl, freckles, light
brown hair. The focus of her grandmother's life.

                        ROSIE
            I just did.

                        KURT
            Let me see.

She shows him her hands.

                        KURT
            Okay. Where's Brian and what's-
            her-name?

                        TOMMY (OS)
            Renee.

                        KURT
            Renee.

                        TOMMY (OS)
            I'll find 'em.

And Tommy goes off down the hall, jerking the camera as
he walks.

                        ROSIE (OS)
            I'm hungry.

> MOM (OS)
> It'll be just a minute, Rosie.
> Linda, wanna get the gravy?

> ROSIE (OS)
> Have any without the lumps? I
> don't like the lumps, Gramma.

Nothing out of the ordinary in the hallway, but as we
move towards the end of the hall we hear some giggles...

> RENEE (OS)
> Come on, Brian, cut it out.

> BRIAN (OS)
> Shush, they'll hear.

> RENEE (OS)
> You're not supposed to be in here,
> anyway.

> BRIAN (OS)
> Who says?

> RENEE (OS)
> Whaddya mean, who says? Your mom
> says. Separate rooms. At least
> 'til we get back to Berkeley.
>   (a beat)
> Ooh, that's good.

The camera's slinking towards a partially open door,
pushing it open to see BRIAN, 20, athletic, on his
knees kissing the stomach of RENEE, 20, a voluptuous
blonde naked from the waist up.

> TOMMY (OS)
> Oh, shit! I'm sorry.

They look up... Brian reaches up with his hand to cover
the lens as Renee turns away, covering her breasts
with her arms. The camera doesn't swing around as
quickly as it probably should...

> RENEE   BRIAN
> Do you mind?   Hey! Get out of here!

> TOMMY (OS)
> Oops! Sorry.

> BRIAN
> You little shit! Gimme that
> thing.

162

The camera backs off fast, maybe gets a touch of the
ceiling, as Brian reaches for it.

                    TOMMY (OS)
          Chill, dude.

                    BRIAN
          I want that tape.

                    TOMMY (OS)
          Be cool! I'll erase it. Relax.
          Here...

He points it to the floor for a sec, then back up at
Renee who's strapping on a bra, her back to the camera.

                    BRIAN
          That better be erasing or I swear
          I'm gonna beat the crap outta you.

                    KURT
          It's erasing. I swear on Dad's
          grave.

                    BRIAN
               (forcefully)
          Don't say that.

                    TOMMY (OS)
               (humbled)
          All right.
               (a beat)
          Mom's starting dinner.

Renee slips on a sweater or a blouse, still holding
Tommy's attention...

                    BRIAN (OS)
          Come on, what're you doing?

                    RENEE
          Get that thing off me, already,
          willya?

                    TOMMY (OS)
          I'm erasing. Just about done.
          Okay...

                    BRIAN
          You're so full of shit. Gimme
          that.

                    TOMMY (OS)
          No, it's done. I swear it.

                    BRIAN
        Lemme see.

                    TOMMY (OS)
        Mom's got dinner on the table.
        Come on, everything'll get cold.

He turns to leave, then whips the camera back, sees
Renee turn toward him, now fully dressed.

                    RENEE
        First live pair, Tommy?

                    TOMMY (OS)
                (embarrassed)
        It was an accident, I swear.

He turns the camera back down the hall towards the
dining room.

                    RENEE (OS)
        Now show me yours. Come on. Be
        fair.

Tommy laughs as camera moves toward dining room...
Brian follows behind.

                    BRIAN (OS)
        Are Melanie and Jaleel here?

                    TOMMY (OS)
        Get real. You know Mel, she'll
        show up just as we sit down. You
        met Jaleel?

                    BRIAN (OS)
        No. You?

                    TOMMY (OS)
        Unh uh.

They're in the dining room now. Kurt, Linda, Mom, and
Rosie are taking their places, pouring water, soft
drinks, maybe wine...

                    TOMMY (OS) (Cont'd)
        But I hear he's--

                    MOM
        --Linda, you sit over there.
        Rosie, you sit by me.

For the next pass, I had to answer to the network's notes, most of which had to do with the aliens — getting them in sooner, having more interaction with them, up the stakes, have them do something, attack the family. We didn't want the aliens exposed so soon, but we did a little work to bring in the idea of the aliens earlier. They wanted the family to feel more terror as early as possible. The first few pages are identical, but I've included them for comparison to future drafts. Changes start on page 6.

. . . . . .

COUNTRY NIGHT

ACT I

DON'T FADE IN:

Just start it cold, close up, right on the face of
TOMMY, 16, who is obviously holding the home video
camera in his hands, looking right into the lens,
trying to figure it out. He pushes it out to arm's
length. We see his hair is short with one side
sculptured. Maybe a gold hoop in one ear. Unbuttoned
long sleeve shirt, t-shirt underneath.

SUPER: In the upper right hand corner of the screen,
the word REC. Just underneath: 0:02:57. The time
will advance in real time throughout.

SUPER: In the lower right hand corner of the screen,
the date: NOV. 23, 1995. The date will remain in the
lower right throughout.

> TOMMY
> Okay, okay. I think I got this
> thing figured out.

> KURT (OS)
> Yeah, right, that's what you've
> been saying for the last half an
> hour.

> TOMMY
> No, the red light's on, this time,
> really.

General cheers and applause from the family...

> TOMMY (Cont'd)
> So, here we go, Thanksgiving at
> the McPherson household.

INT. FARM HOUSE - NIGHT

The camera swings around and focuses on KURT, 25, good
looking, family resemblance to Tommy easy to spot, long
sleeve plaid shirt. Hair a little long, but not
radical. He makes a silly face into the camera as he
sets a large, roasted turkey on the table.

> TOMMY (OS)
> Nice bird.

                    KURT
Thank you.

                    TOMMY (OS)
Like you had anything to do with
it.

                    KURT
I paid for it, jerkoff.

                    TOMMY (OS)
Big whoop.

                    KURT
You wanna see a bird, I'll show
you a bird.

Flips him the bird.

                    MOM (OS)
Come on, boys. Let's not be like
that tonight.

                    KURT
Like what?

                    MOM (OS)
You know like what.

                    TOMMY (OS)
Mom, aren't we going to wait for
Melanie and her boyfriend?

The camera gets off Kurt immediately and takes a quick
tour of the dining room, its table set for Thanksgiving,
including a couple of unlit candles in the center...

...until it falls on MOM, 58, holding a bowl of mashed
potatoes.

Following her is LINDA, 25, good looking but a little
worn, doesn't care much how she looks anymore, as she
brings a shallow baking pan to the table.

                    MOM
                (setting down the
                mashed potatoes)
She'll get here by the time the
turkey's carved. As usual.
Tommy, I thought I told you not to
point that thing at me.

                    TOMMY (OS)

Come on, Mom, ~~just for a couple of minutes.~~ You want your great grandchildren to know what you looked like, don't you?

She gives him a "I don't care," wave of the hand.

                    TOMMY (OS)
                (for the camera's
                benefit)
          That's my mom. The cretin with
          the long hair is my brother, Kurt.
          And the poor woman with the famous
          broccoli casserole is Linda, his
          long suffering wife.

                    KURT
          ~~I'll give you suffering.~~ Rosie?
          Go wash your hands, honey.

Camera pans to ROSIE, 6, a cute girl, freckles, light brown hair. The focus of her grandmother's life.

                    ROSIE
          I just did.

                    KURT
          Okay. Where's Brian and Renee?

                    TOMMY (OS)
          I'll find 'em.

And Tommy goes off down the hall, jerking the camera as he walks.

                    ROSIE (OS)
          I'm hungry.

                    MOM (OS)
          It'll be just a minute, Rosie.
          Linda, wanna get the gravy?

                    ROSIE (OS)
          Have any without the lumps? I
          don't like the lumps, Gramma.

Nothing out of the ordinary in the hallway, but as we move towards the end of the hall we hear some giggles...

                    RENEE (OS)
          You're not supposed to be in here.

                    BRIAN (OS)
          Who says?

                    RENEE (OS)
          Whaddya mean, who says? Your mom
          says. So, until we're back home...
                    (a beat)
          Ooh, that's good.

The camera's slinking towards a partially open door,
pushing it open to see BRIAN, 20, athletic, on his
knees kissing the stomach of RENEE, 20, a voluptuous
blonde naked from the waist up.

                    TOMMY (OS)
          Oh, shit! I'm sorry.

They look up... Brian reaches up with his hand to cover
the lens as Renee turns away, covering her breasts
with her arms. The camera doesn't swing around as
quickly as it probably should...

          RENEE   BRIAN
Do you mind?   Hey! Get out of here!

                    TOMMY (OS)
          Oops! Sorry.

                    BRIAN
          You little shit! Gimme that
          thing.

The camera backs off fast, maybe gets a touch of the
ceiling, as Brian reaches for it.

                    TOMMY (OS)
          Chill, dude.

                    BRIAN
          I want that tape.

                    TOMMY (OS)
          Be cool! I'll erase it. Relax.
          Here...

He points it to the floor for a sec, then back up at
Renee who's strapping on a bra, her back to the camera.

                    BRIAN (OS)
          That better be erasing or I swear
          I'm gonna beat the crap outta you.

Renee slips on a sweater or a blouse, still holding
Tommy's attention...

                    TOMMY (OS)

I'm erasing. Okay, there.

                    BRIAN
You're so full of shit. Gimme
that.

                    TOMMY (OS)
No, it's done. I swear it.

                    BRIAN
Lemme see.

                    TOMMY (OS)
Mom's got dinner on the table.
Come on, everything'll get cold.

He turns the camera back down the hall towards the
dining room. Brian follows behind.

                    BRIAN (OS)
Are Melanie and Jaleel here?

                    TOMMY (OS)
Get real. You know Mel, she'll
show up just as we sit down.

                    KURT
What kind of name is Jaleel,
anyway?

They reach the dining room where Kurt, Linda, Mom, and
Rosie are taking their places, pouring water, soft
drinks, maybe wine...

                    TOMMY (OS)
I don't know, Arab?

                    KURT
Just what we need, a camel jockey
in the family.

                    MOM
Don't tell me you're going to do
that while you eat, Tommy.

                    TOMMY (OS)
I can eat one handed.

                    BRIAN
That's not all he can do one
handed.

                    MOM
Come on boys, not in front of

Rosie.

                    ROSIE
What're they talking about, Mommy?

                    LINDA
Nothing, honey. Just sit down.

                    KURT
Okay, Tommy, that's enough video
for one night, don't you think?

                    TOMMY (OS)
No way. I'm gonna make ten
thousand bucks off America's
Funniest Home Videos.

...suddenly there's a flash of bright light from the
outside, as if lightening has struck the house, but
with no noise. Then all the lights go out.

     TOMMY (OS)   KURT
What the hell was that?   Who turned off the lights?

     RENEE   LINDA
What happened?   I didn't.

     BRIAN   KURT
I don't know. Lightening?   Then who did?

                    TOMMY (OS)
          I didn't hear any thunder.

Kurt strikes a match and lights a candle while Mom
flicks a switch up and down.

                    MOM
Power's out. Microwave must've
blown a fuse or something.

                    KURT
Get a flashlight, Tommy. We'll
check the fuse box.

                    TOMMY (OS)
There's a light on my camera.

                    MOM
Hurry up, I don't want everything
to get cold.

                    KURT
It'll just take a minute, Mom.

This process went on and on for another year until we got to what we thought was going to be the shooting script. By this time, I had focused more on the personal relationships, setting up the conflict between Kurt and his wife, Linda. Notice the introduction of characters both to give the implication of reality and to disparage the "reality."

. . . . . .

THE McPHERSON TAPE

formerly

COUNTRY NIGHT

STORY BY

DEAN ALIOTO

TELEPLAY BY

PAUL CHITLIK

C O N F I D E N T I A L

FOR YOUR EYES ONLY

THIS SCRIPT IS THE PROPERTY OF DICK CLARK FILM GROUP AND MAY NOT BE DISTRIBUTED OR REPRODUCED WITHOUT WRITTEN PERMISSION.

October 3, 1997

THE McPHERSON TAPE

formerly known as

COUNTRY NIGHT

PRODUCTION NOTES:

Except for the interviews, this will look and sound like a
home video.

We will often hear a person speak before we reach him/her,
but when there's time, the camera will go to the speaker and
follow the conversation. People will often not wait for the
other speaker to finish before starting to speak themselves.
Lots of overlapping dialogue. Repetition. Very fast paced.
And, in places, two or even three people will be speaking, or
yelling, at once. This is the real way that people talk.

Camera work will be sometimes jerky, sometimes smooth,
sometimes slow to focus or too dark, sometimes not looking at
anything at all (but not for long) as Tommy runs or does
something that requires his hands.

Swish pans can be just right or way too fast, depending on
the situation and Tommy's level of excitement. The whole
thing should appear as if there are no cuts except in-the-
camera edits, as if shot on one continuous tape. Profanity
will be bleeped, nudity tiled or blurred in post. The camera
never stops, until the end.

THE McPHERSON TAPE

INTRODUCTION TO ACT ONE

COLD OPEN:

FADE SUPER UP FROM BLACK: JASON ARNETT

                             VIDEOMETRICS LABORATORIES

FADE OUT, THEN

INT. VIDEO CONTROL ROOM

Lots of tape decks and monitors, maybe a workbench with some
VHS cassettes on it, one or two of them opened and unspooled.
Sitting with his back to the monitors and workbench, facing
camera is JASON ARNETT, 30'S, glasses, very techie.

                    ARNETT
          The McPherson tape is a fake.
          It's, uh, a pretty incredible
          fake, but I don't think it's
          anything more. The analysis we
          did on the footage showed images
          that were more highly pixilated
          than your normal home videotape.
          A reason for this could be digital
          special effects. Digital effect
          will have more lines of resolution
          than normal consumer videotape, so
          you can see its fingerprints. The
          only way this video could be real
          is if the image videotaped was so
          intense it burned a sharper image
          onto it... That's possible, but
          this would be the first time I've
          seen it.

                            CUT TO:

BLACK.

FADE UP SUPER: SHERIFF KENT TILSON,

                LAKE COUNTY,   *Hortons* — *Reseach*

FADE OUT, THEN   *Wyoming*

INT. SHERIFF'S OFFICE - DAY   (Montero)

This is a rural sheriff's office, nothing fancy. We don't
see the cells in the bg, but we know they're close. The
SHERIFF, 50's, is the kind of man you really trust.

                    SHERIFF TILSON
          I'm not comfortable with a
          statement confirming or denying
          the possibility that the
          McPhersons were abducted by, uh,
          extraterrestrials. My deputy
          found the tape at the McPherson
          place, and the McPhersons haven't
          been heard from since. Beyond
          that, I have no comment.

                                   FADE OUT

ACT ONE

DON'T FADE IN:

Just start it cold, close up, right on the face of TOMMY, 16, who is obviously holding the home video camera in his hands, looking right into the lens, trying to figure it out.

In the b.g. we HEAR an unsure and mistake-riddled version of "Chopsticks" on the piano. All this under...

                    HOST (VO)
          The footage you are about to see
          is known as the McPherson Tape. It
          contains explicit and frightening
          images. Lake County sheriff's
          deputies discovered it in a remote
          farmhouse when they investigated
          a missing persons report. It
          purportedly chronicles the last
          hours of a family just before they
          were abducted by beings that were
          possibly from another world.
          Watch the complete and unedited
          tape and decide for yourself:
          Alien abduction - could it happen?
          Did it happen?

Tommy pushes the camera out to arm's length. We see his hair is short with one side sculptured. Maybe a gold hoop in one ear. Unbuttoned long sleeve shirt, t-shirt underneath.

SUPER: In the lower right hand corner of the screen, the date as it would be supered in a home video camera: NOV. 27, 1997. After five seconds, the date disappears.

                    TOMMY
          Okay, okay. It's working now. I
          got it figured out.

                    KURT (OS)
          Yeah, right, that's what you've
          been saying for the last half hour.

                    TOMMY
          No, the red light's on this time.

The faint music stops for a second as cheers and applause come from the family...

INT./EXT. FARM HOUSE - NIGHT

The music picks up again as the camera swings around, panning
by MOM, 58, gray, glasses, sitting at a piano next to ROSIE,
6, a cute girl, freckles, light brown hair. The focus of her
grandmother's life.

They finish up the four handed "Chopsticks" we've been
hearing in the b.g. Rosie laughs.

                    ROSIE
          That was fun, Gramma.

Mom gives Rosie a little hug and gets up from the piano,
crosses to the kitchen.

The camera lands on KURT, 25, good looking, family
resemblance to Tommy easy to spot, long sleeve plaid shirt.
Hair a little long, but not radical. He makes a silly face
into the camera as he sets a large, roasted turkey on the
table.

                    TOMMY (OS)
          Nice bird, Kurt.

                    KURT
               (bows slightly)
          Thank you.

                    TOMMY (OS)
          Like you had anything to do with
          it.

                    KURT
          Let's see. I paid for it. That
          count?

He laughs.

                    TOMMY (OS)
          Mom, aren't we going to wait for
          Mel and her boyfriend?

The camera gets off Kurt immediately and takes a quick tour
of the dining room, its table set for Thanksgiving, including
several unlit candles in the center...

...until it falls on MOM, 58, holding a bowl of mashed
potatoes.

Following her is LINDA, 25, good looking but a little worn,
doesn't care much how she looks anymore. She brings a
shallow baking pan of candied yams to the table.

Mom sets down the mashed potatoes under...

>   MOM
> She'll get here by the time the
> turkey's carved. Tommy, please --
> don't point that thing at me.

>   TOMMY (OS)
> Come on, Mom. You want your great
> grandchildren to know what you
> looked like, don't you?

She gives him an "I don't care," wave of the hand.

>   LINDA
> I think it's great.

>   KURT
> You would.

Linda's a little stung by this.

>   LINDA
> I wish we'd've taped your dad when
> he was alive.

Mom reacts more than Kurt, acknowledging with a shrug and a
nod that it would have been a good idea.

>   KURT
> Rosie? Go wash your hands, honey.

>   ROSIE
> I just did, Daddy.

>   KURT
> Okay.
>   (to the others)
> Where's Brian and Renee?

>   TOMMY (OS)
> I'll find 'em.

And Tommy goes off down the hall, jerking the camera as he
walks, under...

>   ROSIE (OS)
> I'm hungry.

>   MOM (OS)
> It'll be just a minute, Rosie.
> Linda, wanna get the gravy?

                    ROSIE (OS)
            Have any without the lumps? I
            don't like the lumps, Gramma.

                    MOM (OS)
            You mean the giblets, honey.

WE SEE a few family photos on the walls as Tommy troops down
the hall. The only sounds WE HEAR are Tommy's breathing and
his soft footsteps. It looks a little spooky, like something
bad is going to happen. Then...

As we near the end of the hall WE HEAR some giggles...

Tommy slows down. His footsteps become quieter. The camera
slinks towards a partially open door, pushing it further to
reveal BRIAN, 20, athletic, on his knees kissing the stomach
of RENEE, 20, a voluptuous blonde woman, naked from the waist
up. (We'll tile it.)

                    TOMMY (OS)
            Oh, shit!

(We'll beep "shit," so don't be afraid to say it.)

They look up... Brian reaches up with his hand to cover the
lens as Renee turns away, covering her breasts with her arms.
The camera doesn't swing around as quickly as it probably
should...

            RENEE   BRIAN
        Do you mind?   Hey! Get out of here!

                    TOMMY (OS)
            Oops! Sorry.

                    BRIAN
            You little jerk-off! Gimme that
            thing.

The camera backs off fast, maybe gets a touch of the ceiling,
as Brian reaches for it.

                    TOMMY (OS)
            Chill out, Brian.

                    BRIAN
            I want that tape.

                    TOMMY (OS)
            Ow! Be cool! I'll erase it.
            Relax. Here...

This next draft is the last draft plus dialogue added on set. Since we shot it from start to finish at least five times (I'm pretty certain we shot it twice in one day on more than one occasion), there are several versions of what was actually said. Again, the script is not complete until the final edit, though this was pretty much what the international version was. It can still be found online in a pirated DVD. One day Dick Clark Productions will release it in a director's cut.

In this draft I focused even more on the intra-family relationships, bringing out as much conflict as possible between the brothers and Kurt and his wife, Linda.

· · · · · ·

A. Hunnater.

FINAL DRAFT: OCTOBER 14, 1997
Revised: 10/21/97   (pink)
Revised: 10/24/97   (yellow)
Revised: 10/25/97   (2nd half)
                      (yellow)
Revised: 10/27/97   (goldenrod)
Revised: 10/28/97   (green)
Revised: 10/29/97   (salmon)
Revised: 10/30/97   (gray)
Revised: 10/31/97   (cream)
Revised: 11/2/97   (white)

THE McPHERSON TAPE

formerly

COUNTRY NIGHT

STORY BY

DEAN ALIOTO

TELEPLAY BY

PAUL CHITLIK

C O N F I D E N T I A L

FOR YOUR EYES ONLY

THIS SCRIPT IS THE PROPERTY OF DICK CLARK FILM GROUP AND MAY NOT BE
DISTRIBUTED OR REPRODUCED WITHOUT WRITTEN PERMISSION.

THE McPHERSON TAPE

formerly known as

COUNTRY NIGHT

PRODUCTION NOTES:

Except for the interviews, this will look and sound like a
home video.

We will often hear a person speak before we reach him/her,
but when there's time, the camera will go to the speaker and
follow the conversation. People will often not wait for the
other speaker to finish before starting to speak themselves.
Lots of overlapping dialogue. Repetition. Very fast paced.
And, in places, two or even three people will be speaking, or
yelling, at once. This is the real way that people talk.

Camera work will be sometimes jerky, sometimes smooth,
sometimes slow to focus or too dark, sometimes not looking at
anything at all (but not for long) as Tommy runs or does
something that requires his hands.

Swish pans can be just right or way too fast, depending on
the situation and Tommy's level of excitement. The whole
thing should appear as if there are no cuts except in-the-
camera edits, as if shot on one continuous tape. Profanity
will be bleeped, nudity tiled or blurred in post. The camera
never stops, until the end.

CONTINUED

CONTINUED:

THE McPHERSON TAPE

INTRODUCTION TO ACT ONE

COLD OPEN:

1 FADE SUPER UP FROM BLACK: JASON ARNETT   1

                              VIDEOMETRICS LABORATORIES

FADE OUT, THEN

2 INT.   VIDEO CONTROL ROOM   2

Lots of tape decks and monitors, maybe a workbench with some
VHS cassettes on it, one or two of them opened and unspooled.
Sitting with his back to the monitors and workbench, facing
camera is JASON ARNETT, 30'S, glasses, very techie.

                    ARNETT
          The McPherson tape is a fake. It's,
          uh, a pretty incredible fake, but I
          don't think it's anything more. The
          analysis we did on the footage showed
          images that were more highly
          pixilated than your normal home
          videotape. A reason for this could
          be digital special effects. Digital
          effect will have more lines of
          resolution than normal consumer
          videotape, so you can see its
          fingerprints. The only way this
          video could be real is if the image
          videotaped was so intense it burned
          a sharper image onto it... That's
          possible, but this would be the first
          time I've seen it.

                                        CUT TO:

3 BLACK.   3

FADE UP SUPER: SHERIFF KENT TILSON,

                 LAKE COUNTY, MONTANA

FADE OUT, THEN

ACT ONE

5 DON'T FADE IN: 5

   Just start it cold, close up, right on the FACE of TOMMY, 16,
   who is obviously holding the home video camera in his hands,
   looking right into the lens, trying to figure it out.

   In the b.g. we HEAR an unsure and mistake-riddled version of
   "Chopsticks" on the piano. All this under...

                    HOST (VO)
               The footage you are about to see is
               known as the McPherson Tape. It
               contains explicit and frightening
               images. Lake County sheriff's
               deputies discovered it in a remote
               farmhouse when they investigated a
               missing persons report. It
               purportedly chronicles the last hours
               of a family just before they were
               abducted by beings that were possibly
               from another world. Watch the
               complete and unedited tape and decide
               for yourself: Alien abduction -
                         Did it happen?

   Tommy pushes the camera out to arm's length. We see his hair
   is short with one side sculptured. Maybe a gold hoop in one
   ear. Unbuttoned long sleeve shirt, t-shirt underneath.

   SUPER: In the lower right hand corner of the screen, the
   date as it would be supered in a home video camera: NOV. 27,
   1997. After five seconds, the date disappears.

                    TOMMY (Tooth)
               Okay, okay. It's working now. I got
               it figured out.

                    KURT (OS)
               Yeah, right, that's what you've been
               saying for the last half hour.

                    TOMMY
               No, the red light's on this time.

   The faint music falters and stops for a second as cheers and   *
   applause come from the family...

6 INT./EXT. FARM HOUSE - NIGHT   6

The music picks up again as the camera swings around, panning
some family pictures on the wall, maybe a few athletic
trophies on shelves or the piano. Then it lands on MOM, 58,
gray, glasses, sitting at a piano next to ROSIE, 6, a cute
girl, freckles, light brown hair. The focus of her
grandmother's life.

                    TOMMY (OS)
          Okay, here we have my mom and my niece,
          Rosie, they are away to a wicked)
          version of Chopsticks. on the piano

They finish up the four handed "Chopsticks" we've been
hearing in the b.g. Rosie laughs.

                    ROSIE
          That was fun, Gramma.

                    MOM
          You really played great. honey (You played real good honey) (You played real great honey)
Ad lib some other compliments from various members of the
family.

Mom gives Rosie a little hug.

SFX: DING! (MICROWAVE BELL)

Mom gets up from the piano, crosses to the kitchen. Tommy
follows her... (Tommy Murphy...)
                    TOMMY (OS)
          Mom, tell us about Thanksgiving in
          the McPherson household.

                    MOM
          No, thank you.

But Tommy follows her as she reaches the microwave, takes out
the mashed potatoes under...

                    TOMMY (OS)
          Come on. (Mom)

Mom mugs a little for the camera.

                    MOM
          (Well) What do you want me to say?

                                          CONTINUED

6 CONTINUED: 6

                         TOMMY (OS)
              Whatever comes into your head.

She stirs up the mashed potatoes with a wooden spoon, adds
some salt, etc., under...

                         MOM
              Well, every year we all get together,
              no matter where we're living. You
              kids ____ come ____ home, and your
              father and I... I mean...
                   (she starts to choke
                   up)
              We / ~~have~~ _____ dinner and
              light the Thanksgiving candle.. (Thats it.)
              Okay, no more. Tommy.

Tommy reaches out, pats her on the shoulder, comforts her.

                         TOMMY (OS)
              You okay, Ma?

Hold on the moment, then...

                   Yeah Im fine
                         MOM   (just gotta)
              Go on, Tommy. (I'm okay.) Let me
              finish the potatoes. (No more Tommy)
                   (off)   (Go on Tommy)
And she wipes away a tear with the back of her hand and
continues whipping the potatoes.

                         MOM
                   (continuing)
              Go on.

                         TOMMY (OS)
              Okay.

And the camera swings around and lands on KURT, 25, good
looking, family resemblance to Tommy easy to spot, long
sleeve plaid shirt. Hair a little long, but not radical. He
makes a silly face into the camera as he sets a large,
roasted turkey on the table.

                         TOMMY (OS)
                   (re the turkey)
              Hey, nice bird, Kurt (us)

                                                    CONTINUED

190

6 CONTINUED: (2)   6

                              KURT
                         (bows slightly)
                    Thank you.

                              TOMMY (OS)
                    Like you had anything to do with it.

                              KURT
                    Let's see. I paid for it. That
                    count? (for anything)

He laughs.

                              TOMMY (OS)
                    Oh, yes, Kurt, the bait shop king.

                              KURT
                         (good humoredly)
              Hey Bait's put food on your table all
                    your life, (you little punk.)

                              TOMMY (OS)
                    You mean all this time I've been
                    eating fish bait?

Kurt tries to get pissed off, but can't. He smirks it off.

                              KURT
                    Smart ass.

They both laugh.

                              TOMMY (OS)
                    Mom, aren't we going to wait for Mel
                    and her boyfriend?

The camera gets off Kurt immediately and takes a quick tour
of the dining room, its table set for Thanksgiving, including
several unlit candles in the center...

...until it falls on Mom, carrying the bowl of mashed
potatoes to the table.

Following her is LINDA, 25, good looking but a little worn,
doesn't care much how she looks anymore. She brings a
shallow baking pan of candied yams to the table.

                                                   CONTINUED

6 CONTINUED: (3)   6

Mom sets down the mashed potatoes under...

                         MOM
Oh you know Me. She'll get here by the time the
                    turkey's carved. _____
                    don't point that thing at me any more.

                      TOMMY (OS)
                Sorry, Mom, I just want your great
                grandchildren to know what you looked
                like.

She gives him an "I don't care," wave of the hand.

                       LINDA
             I think its great.

                       KURT
                Oh, yes, he blows his inheritance on
                a video camera, *and you think this* great.
                TOMMY: It wasn't the whole thing.
Linda's a little stung by this.

                       LINDA
                I wish we'd've taped your dad when he
                was alive.
                      (Still)
Mom reacts more than Kurt, acknowledging with a shrug and a
nod that it would have been a good idea.

                      TOMMY (OS)
                        (to Linda)
                Me, too.

             (Rosie?)   KURT   *(Rosie)*
                      Go wash your hands, honey.
                      (its time to)
                       ROSIE
                I just did, Dad.

             (lets see) KURT
                Let me see?
                        (checking her hands)
             Pretty Good. (very good)
                        (to the others)
                Where's Brian and Renee?

                      TOMMY (OS)
                I'll find 'em.

                                        CONTINUED

6 CONTINUED: (4)   6

And Tommy goes off down the hall, jerking the camera as he
walks, under...

                    ROSIE (OS)
          I'm hungry.

                                                  CONTINUED

6 CONTINUED: (5)   6

                    MOM (OS)
          It'll be (ready in a few minutes) Rosie. Linda,
          wanna get the gravy?

                    ROSIE (OS)
          Have any without the lumps?. I don't
          like the lumps, Gramma.

                    MOM (OS)
          You mean the giblets, honey.

WE SEE a few family photos on the walls as Tommy troops down
the hall. As Tommy goes down the hall, poking into rooms...

                    TOMMY (OS)
                    (whispering)
          Coming up, we have my loser brother,
          Brian, and his babe girlfriend,
          Renee.. She is most impressive.
                    (calling quietly)(excellent)
          Bri. Bri... Wherever could he be?
          (where did you get too?) (love of my life where did you go)
As we near the end of the hall WE HEAR some giggles...

                    TOMMY (OS)
                    (continuing;
                    whispering)
          Fornicating in the bathroom.. (Oh dear)
                                       (for shame)
                                       (Naughty, Naughty)
Tommy slows down. His footsteps become quieter. He enters
the dark bedroom and moves toward the crack of light escaping
from the partially opened bathroom door. He stops just
outside the door, and WE HEAR some bits of conversation...

                    RENEE (OS)
          Brian! Come on, give me my shirt
          back.

                    BRIAN (OS)
          Not until you say yes.

                    RENEE (OS)
                    (giggles again)
          I'll think about it. Come on. Brian your mom's in the other
                                                              room.
                    BRIAN (OS)
          Maybe this'll help you decide.

                                                    CONTINUED

6 CONTINUED: (6)   6

                         RENEE
        Brian!

There's silence for a beat, then, a little moan escapes from
Renee. The camera slinks towards the door, pushing it
further to reveal BRIAN, 20, athletic, on his knees kissing
the stomach of RENEE, 20, a voluptuous brunette woman, naked
from the waist up. (We'll tile it.)

They look up... Brian reaches up with his hand to cover the
lens as Renee turns away, covering her breasts with her arms.
The camera doesn't swing around as quickly as it probably
should...

Ohmygod   RENEE (shit!)   BRIAN
           Do you mind?   Hey! Get out of here!

                         TOMMY (OS)
        Oops! Sorry.

                         BRIAN
        You little jerk-off! Gimme that
        thing.

The camera backs off fast, maybe gets a touch of the ceiling,
as Brian reaches for it.

                         TOMMY (OS)
        Chill out, Brian.
          (cool it)

                                                    CONTINUED

And so we see a scene evolve, for better or for worse. In this one, conflict is more pronounced, setting up issues that will dominate as the family takes on the aliens.

. . . . . .

BIBLIOGRAPHY

Ackerman, Hal. *Write Screenplays That Sell: The Ackerman Way*. Los Angeles: Tallfellow Press, 2003.

Bowles, Stephen E., Ronald Mangravite, and Peter Zorn. *The Complete Screenwriter's Manual: A Comprehensive Reference of Format and Style*. Boston: Pearson Longman, 2006.

Brown, Ross. *Byte-Sized Television: Create Your Own TV Series for the Internet*. Studio City: Michael Wiese Productions, 2011.

Bull, Sheldon. *Elephant Bucks: An Inside Guide to Writing for TV Sitcoms*. Studio City: Michael Wiese Productions, 2007.

Douglas, Pamela. *Writing the TV Drama Series: How to Succeed as a Professional Writer in TV*. 3rd ed. Studio City: Michael Wiese Productions, 2007.

Egri, Lajos. *The Art of Dramatic Writing: Its Basis in the Creative Interpretation of Human Motives*. New York: Touchstone Books, 2007.

Field, Syd. *Screenplay: The Foundations of Screenwriting*. Rev. ed. New York: Delta, 2005.

Gelfand, Janna E. *A Practical Guide to Flawless Screenplay Form*. Los Angeles: Get It Right Press.

Goldman, William. *Adventures in the Screen Trade: A Personal View of Hollywood and Screenwriting*. New York: Warner Books, 1983.

Hunter, Lew. *Lew Hunter's Screenwriting 434*. New York: Penguin, 1993.

Hutzler, Laurie. "The Character Map." Emotional Toolbox Website, *http://www.etbscreenwriting.com/character-map/*.
———. *One Hour Screenwriter* (writing course). Emotional Toolbox Website, *http://www.onehourscreenwriter.com/*.

Lerch, Jennifer. *500 Ways to Beat the Hollywood Script Reader: Writing the Screenplay the Reader Will Recommend*. New York: Fireside Books, Simon and Shuster, 1999.

Penniston, Penny. *Talk the Talk: A Dialogue Workshop for Scriptwriters*. Studio City: Michael Wiese Productions, 2009.

Seger, Linda. *Making a Good Script Great*. 2nd ed. Hollywood, CA: Samuel French, 1994.

Strunk, William Jr. and E. B. White. *The Elements of Style*. 4th ed. Boston: Allyn and Bacon, 2000.

Vogler, Christopher. *The Writer's Journey: Mythic Structure for Writers*. 3rd ed. Studio City: Michael Wiese Productions, 2007.

Wallerstein, Michele. *Mind Your Business: A Hollywood Literary Agent's Guide to Your Writing Career*. Studio City: Michael Wiese Productions, 2010.

Walter, Richard. *Screenwriting: The Art, Craft, and Business of Film and Television Writing*. New York: Plume, 2010.

Yoneda, Kathie Fong. *The Script-Selling Game: A Hollywood Insider's Look at Getting Your Script Sold and Produced*. Studio City: Michael Wiese Productions, 2011.

And any screenplay you can get your hands on.

REFERENCES

The author acknowledges the copyright owners of the following motion pictures from which single frames have been used in this book for purposes of commentary, criticism, and scholarship under the Fair Use Doctrine.

Die Hard ©1988. 20th Century-Fox. All Rights Reserved.

Erin Brockovich ©2000. Jersey Films. All Rights Reserved.

How to Marry a Millionaire ©1953. 20th Century-Fox. All Rights Reserved.

In & Out ©1997. Paramount Pictures. All Rights Reserved.

Kiss Kiss, Bang Bang ©2005. Warner Bros. and Silver Pictures. All Rights Reserved.

Pirates of the Caribbean: The Curse of the Black Pearl ©2003. Walt Disney Pictures, Jerry Bruckheimer Productions. All Rights Reserved.

Ratatouille ©2007. Pixar Pictures. All Rights Reserved.

Shakespeare in Love ©1998. Universal Pictures and Miramax Films. All Rights Reserved.

Thelma & Louise ©1991. Pathé Entertainment. All Rights Reserved.

The Cable Guy ©1996. Columbia Pictures. All Rights Reserved.

The Patriot ©2000. Columbia Pictures. All Rights Reserved.

The Sessions ©2012. Such Much Films and Fox Searchlight. All Rights Reserved.

The Wizard of Oz ©1939. Metro-Goldwyn-Mayer. All Rights Reserved.

Two and a Half Men ©2003–. Warner Bros. Television, Chuck Lorre Productions, and The Tannenbaum Company. All Rights Reserved.

ABOUT THE AUTHOR

 PAUL CHITLIK'S writer/producer credits include *The New Twilight Zone, Who's the Boss, Brothers, Amen, Perfect Strangers, Small Wonder, Los Beltrán, They Came from Outer Space, V.I.P.,* and *American Playhouse.* He wrote and produced the first network television movie, *Alien Abduction,* shot on digital video for UPN and produced and directed numerous episodes of *U.S. Customs Classified* and *Real Stories of the Highway Patrol.* Mr. Chitlik has created several pilots as well as written feature films for Rysher, NuImage, Mainline Releasing, and Promark. He wrote, produced, and directed *Ringling Brothers Revealed* for Travel Channel. He has been nominated for a WGA Award and a GLAAD Media Award and has won a Genesis Award for a Showtime Family movie.

He has taught screenwriting in the Professional Program and the MFA program at UCLA; at ESCAC, the film school of the University of Barcelona, Spain, not to be confused with the Autonomous University of Barcelona, where he has also taught in the Masters Program in Screenwriting; and EICTV, the film school of Cuba. He has advised the Chilean film development board (CORFO) on film projects and has served as writer in residence at the Ibermedia Colloquium in Santiago, Chile. He also consults for ScreenAustralia and ScreenWest, Australia. He currently is a clinical assistant professor in screenwriting at Loyola Marymount University's School of Film and Television.

His exclusive rewrite seminars have taken place in Cortona and Cairo Montenotte, Italy; Berkeley and Los Angeles, California; Estanyol, Spain; Ver-sur-Mer and Burgundy, France. He is the author of three novels, including the Berns series of mysteries.

He lives in Sherman Oaks, California, with his wife, a television producer.

INDEX

Action: 2, 5–7, 16, 40, 61, 72, 77, 103

    Films, action: 22

    In subtext: 73

    In sitcoms: 137–138

    Motivating action: 24, 29

    Paragraphs: 74

    Proving premises: 25

    Pushing the: 31

    Revealing character through: 34–35, 47, 55

    Rising: 128

    Scene: 56, 57

    Taking: 39

Akins, Zoe: 32

Albert, Katherine: 32

Alien Abduction: 153–196

Anderson, Jane: x, 33

Annie Hall: 25

Antagonist: 12, 13, 33, 45–49, 55, 62, 66

Apu Trilogy, The: xii

Argo: 43

Aristophanes: 135

Armageddon: 42

Art of Dramatic Writing, The: 23, 26, 197

As Good as It Gets: 39

Avatar: 26, 42

Avengers, The: 35, 42

Bach, Danilo: 82

Barriers: 1, 10, 13–14, 52

Bass, Ron: 129

Bearman, Joshuah: 43

Beat sheet, beatsheet: 11, 53–54, 58, 62, 86–87, 95

    Bike Squad, The: 87

    In Good Company: 146

Belle Epoch: xii

Beverly Hills Cop: 82

Bicentennial Man: 31

Big Chill, The: 23

Big Sleep, The: 65

Bill and Ted's Excellent Adventure: 25

Bird, Brad: 28

Black, Shane: 121–122

Butch Cassidy and the Sundance Kid: 23

Cable Guy, The: 38–39

Camera angles: 126

Camera directions: 127

Cameron, James: 66

Campbell, Joseph: 15

Capobianco, Jim: 28

Capra, Frank: 27

Carrey, Jim: 30, 38–39

CER - Central Emotional Relationship: xiv, 41–43, 142

Chan, Jackie: 102

Chandler, Raymond: 65

Character: viii, xi, xiv, xv, 1–2, 5, 6, 8, 9–14, 16, 23–31, 33–35

    arc: 36–39

Characters, supporting: 12, 79–83

Checklist: 39

Chicken Run: 24

Chinatown: x

China Beach: 30

Clooney, George: 25, 34

Close, Glenn: 5

Coal Miner's Daughter: 36

Colleary, Michael: 127

Comics: 140

Conflict: 11, 17, 23, 31, 45, 49, 52–58, 62, 130

Contact: 72

Coppola, Francis Ford: 64

Count of Monte Cristo, The: 56

Culkin, Macauley: 39

Cusack, Joan: 4

Cutting: 86, 101, 103, 123

Darabont, Frank: 80–81, 85

Defining line, the: 65

de Sousa, Steven: 48, 58

Description: 55, 71–78,101,104

Detonante: 101

Devil with a Blue Dress: 36

Dialogue: 29, 36, 47, 55, 63–69, 77, 102–103, 125, 130, 135

Dick Tracy: 72

Die Hard: 47–48, 58–61

Dillon, Matt: 3

Dirty Harry: 35, 66

Duvall, Robert: 65

Dworet, Lawrence: xi

Egri, Lajos: 23–24, 26

End of Act I: 6, 32, 52, 60–61, 102, 138, 141–142, 145, 147

End of Act II: 17

Epps, Jack, Jr.: 72

Erin Brockovich: 35–36

Eunson, Dale: 32

Face/Off: 129

Faulkner, William: 65

Field, Syd: ix

Final challenge: 8, 9, 14, 37, 49, 52, 62, 101–102, 128, 131, 138,
    141–142, 145, 151

Fink, Harry Julian: 66

Fink, R. M.: 66

Flaw: 2, 6, 10, 13, 26–27, 29, 31, 33–34, 36–37, 39, 46, 59, 79, 138,
    142, 144

Focusing the reader's attention: 126

Foote, Horton: 64

Forrest Gump: 36

Fort Apache: 14, 34

Frances: 31

Frogs, The: 135

Fugitive, The: 33

Gibson, Mel: 25–26

Goal: 1, 2, 4–17, 26–34, 37, 39, 45–46, 49, 52, 55–57, 60, 66, 101, 118,
    138, 140, 143, 145, 147

Godfather II, The: 30, 65

Goldenberg, Michael: 72, 86

Goldwyn, Samuel: 24

Goodrich, Francis: 27

Grammar: 30, 123–125, 130

Green Mile, The: 80, 85

Groundhog Day: 25, 37

Guay, Paul: 30

Hackett, Albert: 27

Hammett, Dashiell: 66

Hanks, Tom: 80

Harry Potter: 72

Hero: 14–16, 18, 20, 31, 33, 37, 59–60, 83

Hero with a Thousand Faces: 15

Hoffman, Dustin: xi

How to Marry a Millionaire: 32

Hunger Games: 32

Hurd, Gale Anne: 66

Huston, John: 66

Hutchison, Don: 81

I

In & Out: 3–7

Inciting incident: 4–6, 8, 10, 16, 32, 51, 60–61, 101, 102, 118, 137, 141, 142, 144, 146

Inglourious Basterds: 49

It Could Happen to You: x

Intouchables, The: 34

It's a Wonderful Life: 27

J

Jules et Jim: xii

Johnson, Nunnally: 32

K

Kazan, Nick: 31

Khouri, Callie: 2, 3, 62

King, Stephen: 80

Kiss Kiss Bang Bang: 121, 122

Kline, Kevin: 3, 4

L

LaGravanese, Richard: 35

Last Year at Marienbad: xii

Lee, Harper: 64

Legal Eagles: 72

Length: 85

Lethal Weapon: 121

Lewin, Ben: 42

Liar Liar: 30

Locale: 85

Low point: 7, 8, 20, 49, 52, 61, 102, 118, 138, 141, 142, 144, 151

Los Olvidados: xii

Lucas, George: 15, 17

M

MacGyver: xi

Making a Good Script Great: 15

Malick, Terrence: 32

Maltese Falcon, The: 66, 91

Mamet, David: 65

Mazur, Steven: 30

McKay, Vince: x

Mercedes-Benz: 124

Merchant of Venice, The: 24

Mi Familia: 36

Midpoint: 6, 33, 37, 61, 82, 92, 98, 102, 117, 118, 138, 141, 142, 145, 150

Million Dollar Baby: 41

Miserables, Les: 49

Montage: 3, 150

Moonlight Kingdom: xii

Morse, David: 81

Motivation: 22

Murphy, Eddie: 82

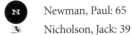

Newman, Paul: 65

Nicholson, Jack: 39

Nicholson, William: 49

Norman, Marc: 51, 52, 63

Newhart, Bob: 6

Objective: 54–55

Ocean's Eleven: 23

Outbreak: xi

Ordinary life: 2, 15, 16, 49, 51, 58, 59, 61, 101, 102, 137, 141, 142, 144, 146

Pacing: 128

Paragraph: 71, 72, 74, 76, 78, 130

Patriot, The: 24–27

Perfect Storm, The: 24–25, 33, 45

Peter Pan: 72

Petrie, Dan, Jr.: 82

Philadelphia Story, The: 41

Pinchot, Bronson: 82

Pinkava, Jan: 28

Pitt, Brad: 7, 37, 49, 82, 132

Platoon: 55–56

Plot: xi, 1, 10, 25, 41

Pool, Robert Roy: xi

Positively True Adventures of the Alleged Texas Cheerleader-Murdering Mom, The: x

Premise: 24–26, 40, 117

Proofread: 124, 129

Protagonist: 2, 4, 5, 8, 10, 11–14, 22–39, 40, 45–47, 49, 51, 52, 57–58, 61–64, 66, 79, 82–83, 86, 101, 118, 128, 144

Punctuation: 73, 123–125, 130

Pursuit of Happyness, The: 39

Puzo, Mario: 65

Ratatouille: 28, 142–143

Remy: 28

Return to normal life: 52, 62, 101

Reversal of Fortune: 31

Reynolds, Debbie: 4

Riesner, Dean: 66

River Wild, The: 39

Rodat, Robert: 26

Romeo and Juliet: 24, 25, 57, 122

Romero: 30

Rudnick, Paul: 3, 4, 5

Scarface: 30

Scene: 10, 11, 51–62, 76, 78, 86, 101, 102, 122, 126, 130

Schiff, Robin: 129

Schmerer, Jim: viii, x, 65

Script: ix, 1, 2, 11, 71, 85, 117, 122, 124

Script Status Report: 117, 132

Secaucus Seven, The: 23

Seger, Linda: 15

Sessions, The: 42

Selleck, Tom: 4, 7

Sequence: 58–62

Seven points: 2–10, 12, 37, 48, 43, 48–49, 51, 62, 136, 139, 140

    of *Pirates of the Caribbean*: 144

    Ratatouille: 142

    Thelma & Louise: 141

Sex and Breakfast: 39

Shakespeare in Love: x, 51, 52, 63, 69

She's Gotta Have It: 36

Shoot the Piano Player: xii

Sitcom: 137–140

Slug line: 122–123

Smith, Will: 39

Social register: 63, 67

Spelling: 73, 123, 125, 130

Spider-Man: 24

Stakes: 12–13

Star Trek: 36

Star Wars: 14, 15, 18, 41, 83

Status: 67–69

Stone, Oliver: 55

Stoppard, Tom: 51–52, 63

Story: xiv–xv, 1 (definition), 2, 6, 10–13, 23, 25, 30, 32, 33, 36–39,

    41–43, 45, 58, 51, 53–56, 58, 73, 76, 77, 79, 83, 86, 103, 128, 130,

    137–140

Streep, Meryl: 39

Structure: 1–11

    Alternative: 15–22

    Dramas: 138–139

    Games: 140

    Graphic novels: 140

    MOWs: 139

    Mythic: 15–22

    One hour: 138–139

    Sitcoms: 137

    Television movies: 139

    Web, The: 139

Stuart, Jeb: 47, 48, 58

Subplots: 12

Subtext: 4, 63–69

    Visual: 73

Supporting Players: 79

Swicord, Robin: 54

Tarantino, Quentin: 49

Talk the Talk: A Dialogue Workshop for Scriptwriters: 69

Terminator, The: 66

Terrio, Chris: 43

Testament: 30

Thelma & Louise: 2–3, 5, 7, 9–10, 23, 32, 37, 41, 61–62, 82

    Seven points of: 141

Titanic: 24

To Kill a Mockingbird: 64, 73

Tootsie: 26, 66

Top Gun: 72

Treasure of the Sierra Madre: 24

Treatment: 11

Tree of Life, The: 32

Trusted adviser: viii, ix, 129

Turning point: 6, 17

    Of a scene: 52

    Of a sitcom: 136

Up in the Air: 34

Van Doren Stern, Phillip: 27

Verdict, The: 65

Vogler, Christopher: ix, 15, 79

Walter, Richard: viii

War of the Worlds: 14

Werb, Mike: 129

When Billie Beat Bobbie: x

Wizard of Oz, The: 14, 18–20, 79–81

Wolpert, Jay: 56, 144

Writers Guild of America, West: viii, x, 130

Writer's Journey, The: ix, 15, 79

Young, John Sacret: 30

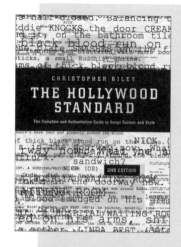

THE HOLLYWOOD STANDARD
2ND EDITION
THE COMPLETE AND AUTHORITATIVE GUIDE TO SCRIPT FORMAT AND STYLE

CHRISTOPHER RILEY

This is the book screenwriter Antwone Fisher (*Antwone Fisher*, *Tales from the Script*) insists his writing students at UCLA read. This book convinced John August (*Big Fish*, *Charlie and the Chocolate Factory*) to stop dispensing formatting advice on his popular writing website. His new advice: Consult *The Hollywood Standard*. The book working and aspiring writers keep beside their keyboards and rely on every day. Written by a professional screenwriter whose day job was running the vaunted script shop at Warner Bros., this book is used at USC's School of Cinema, UCLA, and the acclaimed Act One Writing Program in Hollywood, and in screenwriting programs around the world. It is the definitive guide to script format.

The Hollywood Standard describes in clear, vivid prose and hundreds of examples how to format every element of a screenplay or television script. A reference for everyone who writes for the screen, from the novice to the veteran, this is the dictionary of script format, with instructions for formatting everything from the simplest master scene heading to the most complex and challenging musical underwater dream sequence. This new edition includes a quick start guide, plus new chapters on avoiding a dozen deadly formatting mistakes, clarifying the difference between a spec script and production script, and mastering the vital art of proofreading. For the first time, readers will find instructions for formatting instant messages, text messages, email exchanges and caller ID.

"Aspiring writers sometimes wonder why people don't want to read their scripts. Sometimes it's not their story. Sometimes the format distracts. To write a screenplay, you need to learn the science. And this is the best, simplest, easiest to read book to teach you that science. It's the one I recommend to my students at UCLA."

— Antwone Fisher, from the foreword

CHRISTOPHER RILEY is a professional screenwriter working in Hollywood with his wife and writing partner, Kathleen Riley. Together they wrote the 1999 theatrical feature *After the Truth*, a multiple-award-winning German language courtroom thriller. Since then, the husband-wife team has written scripts ranging from legal and political thrillers to action-romances for Touchstone Pictures, Paramount Pictures, Mandalay Television Pictures and Sean Connery's Fountainbridge Films.

In addition to writing, the Rileys train aspiring screenwriters for work in Hollywood and have taught in Los Angeles, Chicago, Washington D.C., New York, and Paris. From 2005 to 2008, the author directed the acclaimed Act One Writing Program in Hollywood.

$24.95 · 208 PAGES · ORDER NUMBER 130RLS · ISBN: 9781932907636

24 HOURS | **1.800.833.5738** | **WWW.MWP.COM**

DIRECTING ACTORS
CREATING MEMORABLE PERFORMANCES
FOR FILM AND TELEVISION

JUDITH WESTON

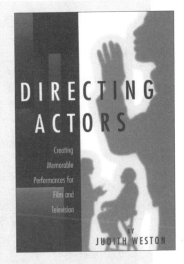

BEST SELLER

Directing film or television is a high-stakes occupation. It captures your full attention at every moment, calling on you to commit every resource and stretch yourself to the limit. It's the white-water rafting of entertainment jobs. But for many directors, the excitement they feel about a new project tightens into anxiety when it comes to working with actors.

This book provides a method for establishing creative, collaborative relationships with actors, getting the most out of rehearsals, troubleshooting poor performances, giving briefer directions, and much more. It addresses what actors want from a director, what directors do wrong, and constructively analyzes the director-actor relationship.

"Judith Weston is an extraordinarily gifted teacher."
> — David Chase, Emmy® Award-Winning Writer,
> Director, and Producer *The Sopranos*,
> *Northern Exposure, I'll Fly Away*

"I believe that working with Judith's ideas and principles has been the most useful time I've spent preparing for my work. I think that if Judith's book were mandatory reading for all directors, the quality of the director-actor process would be transformed, and better drama would result."
> — John Patterson, Director
> *Six Feet Under, CSI: Crime Scene Investigation,*
> *The Practice, Law and Order*

"I know a great teacher when I find one! Everything in this book is brilliant and original and true."
> — Polly Platt, Producer, *Bottle Rocket*
> Executive Producer, *Broadcast News, The War of the Roses*

JUDITH WESTON was a professional actor for 20 years and has taught Acting for Directors for over a decade.

$26.95 · 314 PAGES · ORDER NUMBER 4RLS · ISBN: 9780941188241

24 HOURS | **1.800.833.5738** | **WWW.MWP.COM**

SAVE THE CAT!® GOES TO THE MOVIES
THE SCREENWRITER'S GUIDE
TO EVERY STORY EVER TOLD

BLAKE SNYDER

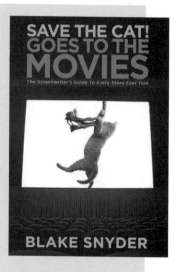

In the long-awaited sequel to his surprise bestseller, *Save the Cat!*, author and screenwriter Blake Snyder returns to form in a fast-paced follow-up that proves why his is the most talked-about approach to screenwriting in years. In the perfect companion piece to his first book, Snyder delivers even more insider's information gleaned from a 20-year track record as "one of Hollywood's most successful spec screenwriters," giving you the clues to write *your* movie.

Designed for screenwriters, novelists, and movie fans, this book gives readers the key breakdowns of the 50 most instructional movies from the past 30 years. From *M*A*S*H* to *Crash*, from *Alien* to *Saw*, from *10* to *Eternal Sunshine of the Spotless Mind*, Snyder reveals how screenwriters who came before you tackled the same challenges you are facing with the film you want to write — or the one you are currently working on.

Writing a "rom-com"? Check out the "Buddy Love" chapter for a "beat for beat" dissection of *When Harry Met Sally...* plus references to 10 other great romantic comedies that will make your story sing.

Want to execute a great mystery? Go to the "Whydunit" section and learn about the "dark turn" that's essential to the heroes of *All the President's Men*, *Blade Runner*, *Fargo* and hip noir *Brick* — and see why ALL good stories, whether a Hollywood blockbuster or a Sundance award winner, follow the same rules of structure outlined in Snyder's breakthrough method.

If you want to sell your script and create a movie that pleases most audiences most of the time, the odds increase if you reference Snyder's checklists and see what makes 50 films tick. After all, both executives and audiences respond to the same elements good writers seek to master. They want to know the type of story they signed on for, and whether it's structured in a way that satisfies everyone. It's what they're looking for. And now, it's what you can deliver.

BLAKE SNYDER, besides selling million-dollar scripts to both Disney and Spielberg, was one of Hollywood's most successful spec screenwriters. Blake's vision continues on *www.blakesnyder.com*.

$24.95 · 270 PAGES · ORDER NUMBER 75RLS · ISBN: 9781932907353

SAVE THE CAT!®
THE LAST BOOK ON SCREENWRITING YOU'LL EVER NEED!

BLAKE SNYDER

BEST SELLER

SAVE THE CAT!
The Last Book On Screenwriting You'll Ever Need!

BLAKE SNYDER

He made millions of dollars selling screenplays to Hollywood and here screenwriter Blake Snyder tells all. "Save the Cat!®" is just one of Snyder's many ironclad rules for making your ideas more marketable and your script more satisfying – and saleable, including:
- The four elements of every winning logline.
- The seven immutable laws of screenplay physics.
- The 10 genres and why they're important to your movie.
- Why your Hero must serve your idea.
- Mastering the Beats.
- Mastering the Board to create the Perfect Beast.
- How to get back on track with ironclad and proven rules for script repair.

This ultimate insider's guide reveals the secrets that none dare admit, told by a show biz veteran who's proven that you can sell your script if you can save the cat.

"Imagine what would happen in a town where more writers approached screenwriting the way Blake suggests? My weekend read would dramatically improve, both in sellable/producible content and in discovering new writers who understand the craft of storytelling and can be hired on assignment for ideas we already have in house."
> – From the Foreword by Sheila Hanahan Taylor, Vice President, Development at Zide/Perry Entertainment, whose films include *American Pie, Cats and Dogs, Final Destination*

"One of the most comprehensive and insightful how-to's out there. Save the Cat!® is a must-read for both the novice and the professional screenwriter."
> – Todd Black, Producer, *The Pursuit of Happyness, The Weather Man, S.W.A.T, Alex and Emma, Antwone Fisher*

"Want to know how to be a successful writer in Hollywood? The answers are here. Blake Snyder has written an insider's book that's informative – and funny, too."
> – David Hoberman, Producer, *The Shaggy Dog* (2005), *Raising Helen, Walking Tall, Bringing Down the House, Monk* (TV)

BLAKE SNYDER, besides selling million-dollar scripts to both Disney and Spielberg, was one of Hollywood's most successful spec screenwriters. Blake's vision continues on *www.blakesnyder.com*.

$19.95 · 216 PAGES · ORDER NUMBER 34RLS · ISBN: 9781932907001

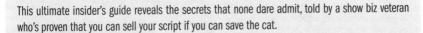

24 HOURS | 1.800.833.5738 | WWW.MWP.COM

THE WRITER'S JOURNEY - 3RD EDITION
MYTHIC STRUCTURE FOR WRITERS

CHRISTOPHER VOGLER

BEST SELLER

See why this book has become an international best seller and a true classic. *The Writer's Journey* explores the powerful relationship between mythology and storytelling in a clear, concise style that's made it required reading for movie executives, screenwriters, playwrights, scholars, and fans of pop culture all over the world.

Both fiction and nonfiction writers will discover a set of useful myth-inspired storytelling paradigms (i.e., "The Hero's Journey") and step-by-step guidelines to plot and character development. Based on the work of Joseph Campbell, *The Writer's Journey* is a must for all writers interested in further developing their craft.

The updated and revised third edition provides new insights and observations from Vogler's ongoing work on mythology's influence on stories, movies, and man himself.

"This book is like having the smartest person in the story meeting come home with you and whisper what to do in your ear as you write a screenplay. Insight for insight, step for step, Chris Vogler takes us through the process of connecting theme to story and making a script come alive."
> – Lynda Obst, producer, *Sleepless in Seattle, How to Lose a Guy in 10 Days*;
> author, *Hello, He Lied*

"This is a book about the stories we write, and perhaps more importantly, the stories we live. It is the most influential work I have yet encountered on the art, nature, and the very purpose of storytelling."
> – Bruce Joel Rubin, screenwriter, *Stuart Little 2, Deep Impact,*
> *Ghost, Jacob's Ladder*

CHRISTOPHER VOGLER is a veteran story consultant for major Hollywood film companies and a respected teacher of filmmakers and writers around the globe. He has influenced the stories of movies from *The Lion King* to *Fight Club* to *The Thin Red Line* and most recently wrote the first installment of *Ravenskull*, a Japanese-style manga or graphic novel. He is the executive producer of the feature film *P.S. Your Cat is Dead* and writer of the animated feature *Jester Till*.

$26.95 · 448 PAGES · ORDER NUMBER 76RLS · ISBN: 9781932907360

24 HOURS | **1.800.833.5738** | **WWW.MWP.COM**

THE MYTH OF MWP

In a dark time, a light bringer came along, leading the curious and the frustrated to clarity and empowerment. It took the well-guarded secrets out of the hands of the few and made them available to all. It spread a spirit of openness and creative freedom, and built a storehouse of knowledge dedicated to the betterment of the arts.

The essence of the Michael Wiese Productions (MWP) is empowering people who have the burning desire to express themselves creatively. We help them realize their dreams by putting the tools in their hands. We demystify the sometimes secretive worlds of screenwriting, directing, acting, producing, film financing, and other media crafts.

By doing so, we hope to bring forth a realization of 'conscious media' which we define as being positively charged, emphasizing hope and affirming positive values like trust, cooperation, self-empowerment, freedom, and love. Grounded in the deep roots of myth, it aims to be healing both for those who make the art and those who encounter it. It hopes to be transformative for people, opening doors to new possibilities and pulling back veils to reveal hidden worlds.

MWP has built a storehouse of knowledge unequaled in the world, for no other publisher has so many titles on the media arts. Please visit www.mwp.com where you will find many free resources and a 25% discount on our books. Sign up and become part of the wider creative community!

Onward and upward,

Michael Wiese
Publisher/Filmmaker

INDEPENDENT FILMMAKERS
SCREENWRITERS
MEDIA PROFESSIONALS

MICHAEL WIESE PRODUCTIONS
GIVES YOU
INSTANT ACCESS
TO THE BEST BOOKS
AND INSTRUCTORS
IN THE WORLD

FOR THE LATEST UPDATES
AND DISCOUNTS,
CONNECT WITH US ON
WWW.MWP.COM

JOIN US ON FACEBOOK   **FOLLOW US** ON TWITTER   **VIEW US** ON YOUTUBE